OPPOSING
VIEWPOINTS®
SERIES

China

Other Books of Related Interest

Opposing Viewpoints Series
America in the Twenty-First Century
Democracy
Globalization
Humanity's Future

Current Controversies Series
Censorship
Developing Nations
Free Speech
Interventionism

At Issue Series
AIDS in Developing Countries
Does the World Hate the United States?
How Should the World Respond to Natural Disasters?
Is North Korea a Global Threat?
U.S. Policy Toward Rogue Nations

"Congress shall make no law . . . abridging the freedom of speech, or of the press."

First Amendment to the U.S. Constitution

The basic foundation of our democracy is the First Amendment guarantee of freedom of expression. The Opposing Viewpoints Series is dedicated to the concept of this basic freedom and the idea that it is more important to practice it than to enshrine it.

China

David M. Haugen, Book Editor

GREENHAVEN PRESS

An imprint of Thomson Gale, a part of The Thomson Corporation

Detroit • New York • San Francisco • San Diego • New Haven, Conn.
Waterville, Maine • London • Munich

THOMSON

TM

GALE

Bonnie Szumski, *Publisher*
Scott Barbour, *Series Editor*
Helen Cothran, *Managing Editor*

LIBRARY OF CONGRESS CATALOGING-IN-PUBLICATION DATA

China / David M. Haugen, book editor.
    p. cm. -- (Opposing viewpoints)
    Includes bibliographical references and index.
    ISBN 0-7377-3389-6 (lib. bdg. : alk. paper) -- ISBN 0-7377-3390-X (pbk. : alk. paper)
    1. China. I. Haugen, David M. 1969– . II. Opposing viewpoints series (Unnumbered)
    DS706.C48855 2006
    951.05--dc22
                                                                    2005052815

Contents

Why Consider Opposing Viewpoints?   11

Introduction   14

Chapter 1: What Are the Most Serious Crises Facing China?

Chapter Preface   20

1. China Faces a Pollution Crisis   22
   Economist

2. China Faces an Energy Crisis   33
   Philip Andrews-Speed

3. China Faces a Health Crisis   42
   Lancet

4. China Faces a Governance Crisis   47
   Minxin Pei

Periodical Bibliography   57

Chapter 2: How Strong Is China's Economy?

Chapter Preface   59

1. China Can Sustain Economic Growth   61
   John Wong and Sarah Chan

2. China Cannot Sustain Economic Growth   69
   Bruce Gilley

3. China's Trade Policies Harm the U.S. Economy   77
   Robert E. Scott

4. China's Trade Policies Do Not Harm the U.S. Economy   85
   Stephen Roach

5. The United States Should Force China to Reduce   **89**
Intellectual Property Theft
Bruce Stokes

6. China Is Taking Action Against Intellectual   **96**
Property Theft
Veronica Weinstein and Dennis Fernandez

Periodical Bibliography   **103**

Chapter 3: Is China a Military Threat?

Chapter Preface   **105**

1. China's Military Is Modernizing   **107**
U.S. Department of Defense

2. The Modernizing of China's Military   **115**
Is Overstated
Ivan Eland

3. China Is a Nuclear Threat   **123**
Thomas M. Kane

4. China Is Not a Nuclear Threat   **134**
Jeffrey Lewis

5. War with China over Taiwan Is Possible   **145**
Richard Halloran

6. War with China over Taiwan Is Unlikely   **157**
Michael O'Hanlon

Periodical Bibliography   **166**

Chapter 4: What Is the State of China's Democratization?

Chapter Preface   **168**

1. The Communist Party Is Promoting Liberal   **170**
Reform in China
Jiang Zemin

2. The Communist Party Is Thwarting Liberal   179
   Reform in China
   Jacques deLisle

3. China Still Suffers from Human Rights Abuses   187
   Amnesty International

4. China Is Making Advances in Human Rights   196
   *Information Office of the State Council of the
   People's Republic of China*

5. China Lacks Media Freedom   205
   Bei Ling and Andrea Huss

6. China's Media Freedom Is Increasing   211
   James Borton

7. China Lacks Religious Freedom   218
   U.S. Department of State

8. China Safeguards Religious Freedom   228
   Chinese Embassy in the United States

Periodical Bibliography   235

For Further Discussion   236

Organizations to Contact   239

Bibliography of Books   244

Index   248

Why Consider Opposing Viewpoints?

> *"The only way in which a human being can make some approach to knowing the whole of a subject is by hearing what can be said about it by persons of every variety of opinion and studying all modes in which it can be looked at by every character of mind. No wise man ever acquired his wisdom in any mode but this."*
>
> John Stuart Mill

In our media-intensive culture it is not difficult to find differing opinions. Thousands of newspapers and magazines and dozens of radio and television talk shows resound with differing points of view. The difficulty lies in deciding which opinion to agree with and which "experts" seem the most credible. The more inundated we become with differing opinions and claims, the more essential it is to hone critical reading and thinking skills to evaluate these ideas. Opposing Viewpoints books address this problem directly by presenting stimulating debates that can be used to enhance and teach these skills. The varied opinions contained in each book examine many different aspects of a single issue. While examining these conveniently edited opposing views, readers can develop critical thinking skills such as the ability to compare and contrast authors' credibility, facts, argumentation styles, use of persuasive techniques, and other stylistic tools. In short, the Opposing Viewpoints Series is an ideal way to attain the higher-level thinking and reading skills so essential in a culture of diverse and contradictory opinions.

In addition to providing a tool for critical thinking, Opposing Viewpoints books challenge readers to question their own strongly held opinions and assumptions. Most people form their opinions on the basis of upbringing, peer pressure, and personal, cultural, or professional bias. By reading carefully balanced opposing views, readers must directly confront new ideas as well as the opinions of those with whom they disagree. This is not to simplistically argue that everyone who reads opposing views will—or should—change his or her opinion. Instead, the series enhances readers' understanding of their own views by encouraging confrontation with opposing ideas. Careful examination of others' views can lead to the readers' understanding of the logical inconsistencies in their own opinions, perspective on why they hold an opinion, and the consideration of the possibility that their opinion requires further evaluation.

Evaluating Other Opinions

To ensure that this type of examination occurs, Opposing Viewpoints books present all types of opinions. Prominent spokespeople on different sides of each issue as well as well-known professionals from many disciplines challenge the reader. An additional goal of the series is to provide a forum for other, less known, or even unpopular viewpoints. The opinion of an ordinary person who has had to make the decision to cut off life support from a terminally ill relative, for example, may be just as valuable and provide just as much insight as a medical ethicist's professional opinion. The editors have two additional purposes in including these less known views. One, the editors encourage readers to respect others' opinions—even when not enhanced by professional credibility. It is only by reading or listening to and objectively evaluating others' ideas that one can determine whether they are worthy of consideration. Two, the inclusion of such viewpoints encourages the important critical thinking skill of objectively evaluating an author's credentials and bias. This evaluation will illuminate an author's reasons for taking a particular stance on an issue and will aid in readers' evaluation of the author's ideas.

It is our hope that these books will give readers a deeper understanding of the issues debated and an appreciation of the complexity of even seemingly simple issues when good and honest people disagree. This awareness is particularly important in a democratic society such as ours in which people enter into public debate to determine the common good. Those with whom one disagrees should not be regarded as enemies but rather as people whose views deserve careful examination and may shed light on one's own.

Thomas Jefferson once said that "difference of opinion leads to inquiry, and inquiry to truth." Jefferson, a broadly educated man, argued that "if a nation expects to be ignorant and free . . . it expects what never was and never will be." As individuals and as a nation, it is imperative that we consider the opinions of others and examine them with skill and discernment. The Opposing Viewpoints Series is intended to help readers achieve this goal.

David L. Bender and Bruno Leone,
Founders

Introduction

*"China's embrace of democracy will be
one of the defining moments of modern
political history, no less significant than
the Russian Revolution of 1917 or the
fall of the Berlin Wall in 1989."*

—Bruce Gilley,
China's Democratic Future

When the Chinese Communist Party took control of
China in 1949, the new leaders promised to draft a liberal constitution and install a democratic government. Democratization has come slowly in China, however, and, in the
eyes of many in the democratic West, has a long way to go.
The Chinese had already witnessed democratic elections in
1912, after revolution toppled the imperial Qing dynasty that
had ruled China for more than two centuries. However, the
nationalist government that replaced the Qing emperor was
fraught with corruption and instability. In an attempt to bring
unity to China in the 1920s, the nationalist leader Sun Yat-sen
decided to join forces with Chinese Communists whose influence among the Chinese people was growing. The recently
formed Soviet Union served as a model of how a progressive-
minded Communist Party could overthrow the monarchy,
champion the working class, and march toward modernity.
Many Chinese believed that the Communists might be able to
modernize China and save it from the economic crisis that
plagued the world in the 1930s.

The promise of modernity, however, did not come about
according to plan. In the late 1920s, Sun Yat-sen's successor,
the nationalist leader Chiang Kai-shek, broke the alliance with

the Communists and hunted them mercilessly. His extermination campaign drove the Communists into China's mountainous hinterlands after World War II. Though the Communist threat to his regime now seemed remote, Chiang could not unify the nation. The peasantry and many intellectuals believed Chiang was simply a new warlord, the kind that had oppressed the country for centuries. His ministers pocketed public funds, and China's industrial profits went mainly to government functionaries. Inflation ran high and was only exacerbated by Chiang's continuing campaign against the Communists. Tired of the tyranny, the people—and much of Chiang's army—stepped aside as the Communists seized the initiative, forcing Chiang and the remnants of the Kuomintang, the nationalist government, to seek haven on the island of Taiwan.

Mao Zedong, the leader who held his faction of Communists together through the years of struggle against the Kuomintang, founded the People's Republic of China on October 1, 1949. He inaugurated the new government—the new nation—during a mass celebration in Tiananmen Square in Beijing. Mao then began to stabilize China. His government, which was only partially made up of Communists, stopped inflation and instituted land reforms that parceled farmland out to individual farmers. The new administration promised business leaders that private ownership of China's industries would continue in an effort to get the economy moving forward after so many years of social unrest. The progressive programs led most Chinese to believe that democratic political reform was just around the corner. It was not to be.

While the new government approved a constitution that promised equality under law, a host of civil liberties, and free, democratic elections, Mao was formulating other schemes. As author and analyst Bruce Gilley writes in *China's Democratic Future*, "Against the advice of [government] planners, he made the Forbidden City [the seat of China's imperial rulers] his home and hoisted his portrait onto the rostrum over Tiananmen Square. Whatever his avowals of support for democracy, they quickly proved expedient in the face of the autocratic temptation." Mao quickly discarded the results of elections, turned private enterprise into state controlled industry, and collectivized the private farms into communal organizations. He alone became the voice of the state and suppressed or eliminated those who had different views. Mao professed that his strategy was to bolster China's overall economic production with the aim of bettering the lives of all Chinese. To this end, he initiated five-year plans that compelled agriculture and industry to meet production goals that, for Mao, would signal China's progress and also show the world that Chinese communism could be a model for social change. The cost of progress, however, was a ruthless bloodletting and widespread famine. Chinese experts estimate that as many as 70 million Chinese died under Mao's regime. Many were killed in Mao's quest to silence dissident voices. At least 20 million were victims of starvation, a result of poor agricultural production under Mao's collectivization program.

When Mao Zedong died in 1976, democracy and liberal reform had been put on hold in China for nearly three decades. Deng Xiaoping succeeded Mao as leader of the Communist Party in 1978, and the hope of reform again arose in the hearts of the Chinese. Though a loyal disciple of Mao, Deng recognized that his teacher's methods were leading the nation to ruin. Deng witnessed the growth of free markets in Hong Kong, Singapore, and Taiwan, while watching mainland China's Communist government-planned economy shrivel. He immediately disbanded the collective farms and allowed industry some self-control. Both sectors still had to contribute to government quotas, but the remainder of their profits could be used to further their own endeavors. In addition, Deng's administration tolerated some free enterprise, leading mainlanders and foreigners to believe that the government might loosen its reins over the economy—and perhaps over the society as a whole.

Deng's progressive policies, however, stopped short of effecting real democratic change. Just as under Mao, Communist Party leaders believed that economic growth, not democratic reform, would improve Chinese society. The Communists were therefore satisfied with giving the Chinese a better standard of living without allowing them the right to vote. In fact, the party advocated that democracy had failed China and that disturbing the status quo would only have disastrous economic repercussions. Deng's successors have maintained his policies (even enshrining his winning reforms as "Deng Xiaoping Thought") against all challenges. Jiang Zemin put down student pro-democracy demonstrations in Tiananmen Square in 1989, and Hu Jintao, China's current chief executive, has fought off foreign pressures—especially from the United States—to link economic freedom with improving human rights and civil liberties.

Deng's successors have, however, made concessions to liberalization. Jiang opened membership in the Communist Party to private entrepreneurs—capitalists who, from the most conservative Communist ideology, would have the least stake in fighting for the rights of the workers. And Hu has striven to make China's government more open and accountable—especially in the wake of the bureaucracy's failure to handle the public health threat posed by the spread of SARS (severe acute respiratory syndrome) in 2003. The focus of their attention nevertheless remains on the economy. Since China's admission to the World Trade Organization in 2001, the Chinese have substantially increased export revenue through trade with a host of foreign nations. Indeed, as Bruce J. Dickson notes in his book *Red Capitalists in China*, many Chinese and foreign observers are content with recent economic reform, hoping that "by expanding the role of market forces, increasing the scope of privatization, and integrating China into the international community, pressures for democratization will become irresistible."

The Chinese Communist Party continues to claim that expanding economic freedoms and minor political concessions are evidence that China is moving toward democratization. Few Westerners, however, see a clear connection, but they hope economic reform is a step in the right direction. The debate concerning whether China will eventually embrace Western-style democracy informs many of the viewpoints in the following chapters of *Opposing Viewpoints: China:* What Are the Most Serious Crises Facing China? How Strong Is China's Economy? Is China a Military Threat? What Is the State of China's Democratization? Although addressing many controversies—from China's military strength to China's environmental problems—the authors acknowledge the importance of understanding China's political agenda and the implications of its avowed democratization. Political reform seems to weigh heavily on all aspects of Chinese society in the early twenty-first century, and the Chinese people as well as the United States and other foreign powers wait anxiously to see what will come. Yet, as Gregory C. Chow, a professor of political economy, cautions in his book *Knowing China,* "In observing the progress towards a more democratic government in China, one should expect it to be a slow process." Chow notes that it took the United States 200 years to develop a more democratic government. "The progress in developing a Chinese democracy," he assures, "cannot be very much faster."

OPPOSING
VIEWPOINTS®
SERIES

What Are the Most Serious Crises Facing China?

Chapter Preface

In the late 1950s and early 1960s, when Mao Zedong ruled China, famine was widespread. Much of this famine could be blamed directly on Mao's insistence on the practice of collective farming. Bureaucratic oversight of collective farms fostered corruption, which ultimately crippled agricultural production. An estimated 30 million Chinese fell victim to food shortages under Mao's leadership. The situation was redressed in the 1970s when Deng Xiaoping ascended to power and steered China into an era of reform. Deng broke up the communes and dismantled the bureaucracy, increasing food production.

When the Deng era came to a close in 1989, some analysts feared the worst for China. Expecting that subsequent administrations would not be as progressive as Deng's, Lester Brown, the president of Worldwatch Institute, published a dire and cautionary report in 1995 entitled *Who Will Feed China?* Brown predicted that because of China's rising population— already the world's largest—and its rapid industrialization, which was ruining the agricultural environment, the nation would soon be unable to feed itself. As a result, Brown calculated, China would be forced to import massive amounts of grain, which would in turn drive up food prices worldwide. Many Western media outlets latched on to Brown's warning and furthered the notion that China would unbalance world food distribution.

Fortunately for China—and the world—Brown's prophecy did not come true. The Chinese government has vast grain stores that keep the population fed through times of shortage. These resources even allowed China to export grain during the 1990s when the world's grain harvest was low. In addition, the "one couple, one child" population control policies have kept China's population from experiencing exponential growth, making it easier for the government to meet the dietary needs of its expanding population. These measures disproved Brown's dire predictions. In fact, according to the UN Food and Agriculture Organization, the average food availability in China remained constant through the 1990s and early 2000s. Ultimately, Western fears proved to be exaggerated, and China's government policies helped the nation avert a potential crisis.

In the following chapter Western critics suggest other looming crises that may thwart China's social and economic progress. Whether these crises are also examples of overstated Western alarmism or whether the predictions will materialize with calamitous consequences is yet to be seen as China steams forward into the new millennium.

> *"China's relationship with its environment has long been uneasy. For centuries, the country's rulers subjugated their surroundings rather than attempting to live in harmony with them."*

China Faces a Pollution Crisis

Economist

In the following viewpoint the Economist, *a British news journal, claims that China suffers from severe environmental pollution. The high levels of pollution are the result of the nation's industrial expansion and the growth of its utilities and other services catering to the demands of China's huge population, the authors argue. The* Economist *also maintains that China's attempts to curb waste and alter environmental policies have been hampered by government bureaucracy. While the journal recognizes that some improvements are likely, given increased foreign and domestic concern, the* Economist *holds that China's pollution will remain a serious problem for years to come.*

As you read, consider the following questions:

1. According to the article, why is most trash in China "wet" (i.e., not solid)?

2. As the *Economist* reports, how many of the world's top-twenty most polluted cities are in China?

3. Why are local environmental protection bureaus largely ineffective in China, according to the *Economist?*

Plugging a cigarette into his mouth, He Shouming runs a nicotine-stained fingernail down a list of registered deaths in Shangba, dubbed "cancer village" by the locals. The Communist Party official in this cluster of tiny hamlets of 3,300 people in northern Guangdong province, he concludes that almost half the 11 deaths among his neighbours [in 2004], and 14 of the 31 [in 2003], were due to cancer.

Mr He blames Dabaoshan, a nearby mineral mine owned by the Guangdong provincial government, and a host of smaller private mines for spewing toxic waste into the local rivers, raising lead levels to 44 times permitted rates. Walking around the village, the water in the streams is indeed an alarming rust-red. A rice farmer complains of itchy legs from the paddies, and his wife needs a new kettle each month because the water corrodes metal. "Put a duck in this water and it would die in two days," declares Mr He.

Poisons from the mines are also killing the village's economy, which depends on clean water to irrigate its crops, says Mr He. Rice yields are one-third of the national average and nobody wants to buy the crop. Annual incomes here have been stuck at less than 1,500 yuan [$180] per person for a decade, almost three times lower than the average in Guangdong province. The solution to Shangba's nightmare would be a local reservoir, but that idea was abandoned after various tiers of government squabbled over the 8.4m [million] yuan cost.

Some 200km [124 miles] farther south and several decades into the future sits the Taihe landfill plant. Built for 540m yuan by Onyx, a waste-management company that is part of Veolia, a French utility, it has handled all of Guangzhou city's solid waste for the past two years [since about 2002]. Each hour 140 trucks snake into the site, bringing 7,000 tonnes [roughly 7,716 U.S. tons] of rubbish a day from the 9.9m inhabitants of Guangdong's capital. In October [2004] delegates from 300 other municipalities will visit Taihe, promoted by central government as a role model of technology.

Smart cards record each truck's load, since Onyx charges by weight. Unrippable German fabric lines the crater into which the waste is dumped, stopping leachate—a toxic black liquid—from leaking into the groundwater, as it does at almost all Chinese-run sites. Most landfill in China is wet (solid rubbish, such as old TVs, is scavenged), and the Taihe plant collects a full 1,300 tonnes [1,433 U.S.] of the black liquid daily. Chemical and filtration systems to neutralise it are its biggest cost. Expensive too is the extraction equipment to gather another by-product, methane gas, which Onyx plans to feed into generators that will supply electricity to the local grid. Finally, the waste is topped off with plastic caps, deodorised and landscaped, while a crystal-clear fountain at the entrance tinkles with the cleaned-up leachate.

Political and Institutional Obstacles

The extremes represented by Shangba and Taihe explain why it is difficult to get an accurate picture of China's pollution. In a country where data are untrustworthy, corruption rife and the business climate for foreigners unpredictable, neither the cause of Shangba's problems nor the smooth efficiency of Taihe are necessarily what they seem. As with many other aspects of China's economic development, rapid progress and bold experiments in some areas are balanced by bureaucratic rigidity and stagnation in others.

Certainly, awareness of China's environmental problems is rising among policymakers at the highest level—reflected in a new package of right-sounding initiatives like a "green GDP [gross domestic product]" indicator to account for environmental costs. So is the pressure, both internal and international, to fix them. But while all developing economies face this issue, there are historical, political and institutional reasons why it will be a long and complicated process in China. There is some cause for optimism, not least an influx of foreign technology and capital. But progress on pollution is unlikely to be as rapid or uniform as the government and environmentalists desire.

Nor should it necessarily be. China's need to lift so many people out of poverty (the country's average annual income per head has only just breached $1,000), holds the edge over long-term considerations like sustainable development. The priorities of environmental activists, both foreign and Chinese, almost never reflect this.

Greenpeace lobbies for China to invest in wind farms, an unrealistic answer to the country's power needs, while environmentalists from rich countries naively tell aspiring Chinese to eschew their new cars and air-conditioners.

Water Pollution

That is not to deny the huge scale of China's environmental challenges. Water and waste pollution is the single most serious issue. Pan Yue, deputy head of the State Environmental Protection Administration (SEPA), the country's environmental watchdog ministry, calls it "the bottleneck constraining economic growth in China". Per head, China's water resources are among the lowest in the world and concentrated in the south, so that the north and west experience regular droughts. Inadequate investments in supply and treatment infrastructure means that even where water is not scarce, it is rarely clean. Around half the population, or 600m people, have water supplies that are contaminated by animal and human waste.

In late July [2004], an environmental disaster occurred on the Huai river, one of China's seven big rivers. A 133km-long [82 mile] black and brown plume swept along the river killing millions of fish and devastating wildlife. According to Mr Pan, the catastrophe occurred because too much water had been taken from the river system, reducing its ability to clean itself. Others say that numerous factories dump untreated waste directly into the water.

As for used water, with a national daily sewage rate of around 3.7 billion tonnes [4 billion U.S.], China would need 10,000 waste-water treatment plants costing some $48 billion just to achieve a 50% treatment rate, according to Frost & Sullivan, a consultancy. SEPA found over 70% of the water in five of China's seven major river systems was unsuitable for human contact. As more people move into cities, the problem of household waste is becoming severe. Only 20% of China's 168m tonnes [185 million U.S.] of solid waste per year is properly disposed of.

Air Quality and Environmental Erosion

The air is not much better. "If I work in your Beijing, I would shorten my life at least five years," Zhu Rongji told city officials when he was prime minister in 1999. According to the World Bank, China has 16 of the world's 20 most polluted cities. Estimates suggest that 300,000 people a year die prematurely from respiratory diseases.

The main reason is that around 70% of China's mushrooming energy needs are supplied by coal-fired power stations, compared with 50% in America. Combined with the still widespread use of coal burners to heat homes, China has the world's highest emissions of sulphur dioxide and a quarter of the country endures acid rain. In 2002, SEPA found that the air quality in almost two-thirds of 300 cities it tested failed World Health Organisation standards—yet emissions from rocketing car ownership are only just becoming an issue. Hopes that China will "leapfrog" the West with super-green cars are naive, since dirty fuel messes up clean engines and the high cost of new cars keeps old ones on the road. Sun Jian, the second-ranking official at Shanghai's environmental protection bureau, estimates that 70% of Shanghai's 1m cars do not even reach the oldest European emission standards.

Percentage Point Contribution to GDP Growth by Each Expenditure Category

Year	GDP Growth Rate (%)	Consumption (%)	Gross Fixed Investment (%)	Net Exports (%)
1981	5.3	5.7	-1.0	0.6
1982	12.1	6.8	3.7	1.6
1983	9.6	6.2	4.1	-0.7
1984	12.4	7.5	5.7	-0.8
1985	11.3	7.6	8.4	-4.7
1986	10.2	5.5	3.3	1.4
1987	10.6	5.4	2.6	2.6
1988	11.3	7.6	4.9	-1.2
1989	2.9	2.3	0.7	-0.1
1990	5.2	1.2	0.03	4.0
1991	8.9	5.2	3.3	0.4
1992	12.7	7.7	6.7	-1.7
1993	16.5	6.4	13.4	-3.3
1994	13.9	7.3	3.1	3.5
1995	9.7	5.3	3.9	0.5
1996	10.2	7.1	2.5	0.6
1997	8.7	4.7	2.0	2.0
1998	8.0	5.3	2.4	0.3
1999	6.7	5.6	2.1	-1.0
2000	8.6	5.7	3.1	-0.2

Consumption refers to personal or household consumption plus government consumption. Investment refers to investment by both the private and public sectors.

Computed from data in *China Statistical Yearbook,* using 1978 as the base year (1978=100). GDP growth rates (listed in table) differ from the official figures due to statistical discrepencies using the GDP by expenditure approach.

Lin Yifu, "Export and Economic Growth in China: A Demand-Oriented Analysis," China Center for Economic Research, Peking University, Paper No. C2002002, May 23, 2002.

Farmland erosion and desertification resulted in Beijing being hit with 11 sandstorms in 2000, prompting Mr Zhu to wonder whether the advancing desert might force him to relocate the capital. A year later, the yellow dust clouds were so extensive that they raised complaints in South Korea and Japan and travelled as far as America. A partial logging ban and massive replanting appear to have reversed China's deforestation, but its grass and agricultural land continue to shrink.

Resources Are Unable to Support the Population

Adding it all up, the World Bank concludes that pollution is costing China an annual 8–12% of its $1.4 trillion GDP in direct damage, such as the impact on crops of acid rain, medical bills, lost work from illness, money spent on disaster relief following floods and the implied costs of resource depletion. With health costs escalating, that figure will increase, giving rise to some grim prognoses that growth itself will be undermined. "Ignored for decades, even centuries, China's environmental problems have the potential to bring the country to its knees economically," argues Elizabeth Economy, author of "The River Runs Black", a new book on China's pollution.

SEPA's Mr Pan is gloomier still: "Our natural resources will soon be unable to support our population." His predecessor Qu Geping, the first head of China's National Environmental Protection Agency (SEPA's forerunner) in 1985, believes that while the official goal of quadrupling 2002 GDP by 2020 can be "healthily achieved", if nothing is done about the environment, economic growth could grind to a halt.

But China's relationship with its environment has long been uneasy. For centuries, the country's rulers subjugated their surroundings rather than attempting to live in harmony with them. Mao declared that man must "conquer nature and thus attain freedom from nature". In the past two decades, the toll extracted by China's manufacturing-led development and the sheer scale of its 9%-a-year economic expansion has only increased.

Ambitious but Thwarted Cleanup Goals

This has spurred the government into belated action. In 1998, Mr Zhu elevated SEPA to ministerial rank and three years later the 10th Five-year Plan for Environmental Protection set ambitious emission-reduction targets and boosted environmental spending to 700 billion yuan ($85 billion) for 2001–05—equivalent to 1.3% of GDP, up from 0.8% in the early 1990s (though still below the 2% suggested by the World Bank). A legal framework has been created. And the rhetoric has changed too, with Hu Jintao and Wen Jiabao, the current president and prime minister, now stressing balanced development rather than all-out economic growth.

Beijing's good intentions, however, have so far had only limited impact, thanks to the vast, decentralised bureaucracy through which it is forced to govern such a huge country. As Ken Lieberthal, a China expert at the University of Michigan, explains: "Much of the environmental energy generated at the national level dissipates as it diffuses through the multi-layered state structure, producing outcomes that have little concrete effect."

SEPA, the government's chosen weapon in the fight against pollution, is under-resourced despite its enhanced status, with little money and just 300 central staff. In the capital, it must battle for influence with other agencies, such as the Construction Ministry that handles water and sewage treatment. Bureaucratic rivalries mean there is no co-operation and no sharing of the (often patchy) data that are collected with limited funds, observes Bruce Murray, the Asian Development Bank's [ADB's] representative in China.

Around the country, SEPA's branches, known as Environmental Protection Bureaus, are supposed to monitor pollution, enforce standards and collect fines. But they are more in thrall to local governments—whose priorities are to maintain growth and employment in their jurisdiction—than to the head office in Beijing. It is no rarity, therefore, to find a bureau imposing a fine on a dirty local enterprise (thus fulfilling its duty), but then passing the money on to the local administration, which refunds it to the company via a tax break. "The environmental management system needs real reform," says Ma Jun, an environmental scholar. "The bureaus depend on the local government for their salaries and pensions. How can they enforce regulations against the local government?" Mr Pan complains that SEPA cannot effectively push through central edicts because it does not directly employ environmental personnel at the local level. Mr Sun at the Shanghai bureau says that SEPA has given him only 300 people with which to police 20,000 factories.

Ineffectual Measures

SEPA's impotence is one reason why penalties, even when it can impose them, remain laughably light. Mr Sun says the maximum he can fine a polluting company in Shanghai—a model city when it comes to the environment—is 100,000 yuan or about $12,000. But just as fundamental is that China lacks an understanding of the concept that the polluter should pay. "The legacy of the old, centrally planned economy is that electricity and water are treated as free goods or goods to be provided at minimal cost," says the ADB's Mr Murray. Since the utilities cannot pass on the costs of cleaner water or lower power-station emissions to consumers, they fight any drive for higher standards and conservation tooth and nail. Even the central government is unwilling to impose price rises in basic services that could spark public unrest.

Water is an example. While customer tariffs have been raised in showcase cities, such as Beijing and Dalian in the north-east, water remains stunningly cheap in China. According to the World Bank, water for agriculture, which makes up three-quarters of the total used, is priced at 0.03 yuan (0.4 cents) per cubic metre [1.3 cubic yards], or about 40% of cost. More than half is lost in leaky irrigation systems. Meanwhile, the cost of more modern services, such as Guangzhou's solid-waste disposal, is entirely borne by the government.

Without the introduction of realistic pricing, China will not be able to afford to clean up its pollution, particularly the cost of enough foreign technology. Yet a system allocating the costs to the polluter will be hard to introduce and enforce. Even in Hong Kong, the territory's environment minister Sarah Liao concedes there is no tradition of having consumers bear the full costs of environmental regulations.

Ms Liao can also testify to the mainland's ambivalent attitude when it comes to letting outsiders help. She started looking into how the Pearl River delta's pollution was affecting Hong Kong back in 1999, but her requests to start monitoring emissions were repeatedly rebuffed even when she offered to pay for the equipment. Data collection finally started this year [2004]. For Thames Water, a British utility that is now a part of Germany's RWE [a utility conglomerate], the experience was much worse. In June [2004], Thames pulled out of a $73m advanced waste-water treatment plant it had built and was running in Shanghai, after the central government ruled that the fixed annual 15% return it had negotiated was now illegal.

Optimism for the Future

There is no need to be unremittingly gloomy about China's environment, nevertheless. As developing countries get richer, they tend to pollute less. Nationally in China, discharges of chemical oxygen have declined over the past three years, those of industrial dust have stabilised and sulphur-dioxide emissions had been on the downtrend until 2003 when energy shortages increased demand for sulphurous coal. Most east-coast cities are enjoying more sunny days and the pollution load in the rivers is falling. Environmentally, in many places, China may have passed its nadir.

The government is increasing environmental spending and the more concerned attitude of the top leadership could filter down the hierarchy if the performance of officials starts being measured partly on environmental criteria, as Mr Qu hints it might. But the bigger incentive is that Beijing is under pressure to do more, partly from domestic public opinion. As urban Chinese see their material wealth increase, more are caring about the environment, while the concerns of the poor are increasingly being channelled by green non-governmental organisations. Though these remain extremely weak—few have more than a handful of members and all need government affiliation—Mr Wen said recently he suspended plans for the construction of 13 dams along the Nu river in Yunnan province partly because of the concerns outlined by such groups.

External pressure is even greater. Despite reservations, foreign companies are flocking to China, scenting a fast-growing market for their environmental technologies and skills. International agencies are tying funds to environmental criteria, while foreign governments are beginning to complain about China's dust storms and greenhouse-gas emissions. All this will help spread best practices. Beijing is fast cleaning up ahead of the 2008 Olympics, moving out factories and introducing clean-vehicle technology: a new premium is being placed on global respectability. Of course, environmental problems and their huge costs will dog China for many years. In a country where the public is not free to speak, too many courts are toothless and environmental groups remain on a tight leash, it will be hard to know if the government's avowedly green policies are being implemented. But China deserves credit for its attempts to clean itself up. The balance between sustainable development and economic growth will have to be continuously adjusted in the future. Right now, China is probably moving in the right direction.

> "[The] weaknesses in China's current energy policy can be traced primarily to the absence of an Energy Ministry or equivalent strong and well-staffed agency responsible for energy policy."

China Faces an Energy Crisis

Philip Andrews-Speed

Philip Andrews-Speed, director of the Centre for Petroleum, Energy, and Mineral Law and Policy at the University of Dundee, Scotland, is the author of Energy Policy Regulation in the People's Republic of China. *In the following viewpoint Andrews-Speed argues that China's energy output has not caught up with demand and therefore the country must import much of its energy. If this trend continues, he maintains, China will face an energy crisis. To allay the problem, Andrews-Speed claims, China must become less dependent on coal, which is inefficiently mined in China and provides less energy than oil or gas.*

As you read, consider the following questions:

1. According to Andrews-Speed, how many times greater is China's rate of increase in energy demand over that of the rest of the world?

2. What two indigenous energy resources were empha-

Philip Andrews-Speed, "China's Energy Woes: Running on Empty," *Far Eastern Economic Review,* June 2005. Copyright © 2005 by the *Far Eastern Economic Review.* Reproduced by permission of Copyright Clearance Center, Inc.

sized in the 1990s to try to counter China's growing
need to import energy?

3. In the author's view, why have the knowledgeable man-
agers of state-owned energy industries been less able to
influence energy policies since the late 1990s?

China faces two pressing sets of energy policy challenges.
The first relates to the immediate need to improve management and coordination of the nation's energy supply. Since
[2003] economic growth has been running at about 9% per
annum. Meanwhile energy demand was up 15% annually
while oil imports grew at 30% per year. Electrical power shortages are widespread, and transport bottlenecks constrain the
ability of the industry to move both coal and oil to where
they are needed.

The second set of challenges is longer-term in nature and
concerns the continuing inability of China's government to
formulate a coherent energy policy which could provide the
basis for the effective management of the energy sector and its
environmental consequences.

Energy Growth Rates Are Not Sustainable

China's energy sector has a number of intrinsic weaknesses.
These include a shortage of domestic oil and gas reserves relative to current and future demand, and a geographic mis-
match between the location of primary energy resources and
the main centers of demand. These deficiencies are being addressed by increasing the level of energy imports and by building long-distance energy transmission infrastructure.

Yet two more profound weaknesses have to be tackled in a
systematic manner, beginning with the issue of overall efficiency of production and use of energy. During the 1980s and
1990s the energy intensity in China declined, reflecting a sustained enhancement of the efficiency with which the country
used energy. Over this period, economic growth was running

at 5% to 10% per year, and the annual rise in energy consumption lay in the range 5% to 8%. Energy intensity, that is the amount of energy used for each unit of GDP [gross domestic product], declined at an average rate of 5% to 6% per year. Today, given the double-digit increase in energy demand over the last two years, it is clear that 20 years of improvements in energy efficiency have been reversed.

Current rates of growth in energy consumption are not sustainable, not least because of the very high rate of investment required to produce, transform and deliver such quantities of energy. China is now the world's second largest consumer of energy, accounting for some 12% of global energy demand, but its rate of increase of demand is some four to five times that for the rest of the world. So what happens in China's energy sector affects us all.

The Drawbacks of Dependence on Coal

The second aspect of China's energy sector which must be addressed by any new energy policy is its continuing dependence on coal. China is the world's largest consumer of coal, accounting for more than 30% of global coal consumption. Further, coal continues to provide some 65% of China's primary energy demand. While such dependence on coal is not necessarily a curse, it has two mutually reinforcing drawbacks: low energy efficiency and pollution.

The heat value of a unit weight of coal is intrinsically less than that for oil and gas, and the recovery rates for many of China's coal mines are low, meaning that much of the country's coal resource is left in the ground, never to be recovered. Furthermore, the efficiency of appliances which use coal in China continues to be substantially lower than the average in OECD [Organisation for Economic Co-operation and Development] countries. Progress has been slow in enhancing the efficiency of consumer electrical appliances and implementing building codes which reduce heat losses. Finally, the continuing low level of end-user prices has failed to provide consumers withincentives to save energy.

As a consequence of all these deficiencies, China is mining, transporting and burning substantially more coal than is strictly necessary. This in turn exacerbates environmental damage, which can be felt locally, regionally and globally.

The government must either find a way to dramatically reduce the country's dependence on coal, or it must adopt the best available technologies and practices to enhance the efficiency and cleanliness with which coal is mined and transformed into energy. Both options necessarily involve huge costs. Given the large size of China's coal resources, it is most likely that the government will prefer the second option. The risk remains that policy paralysis or a failure to effectively implement new policy will result in the continuation of the current trend to use ever increasing amounts of coal, with little improvement in either efficiency or cleanliness.

Lack of a Clear Policy

China's energy policy has traditionally consisted of an aggregate of targets and objectives for investment, production and consumption for each individual industry such as coal, oil, gas and electrical power. Despite the array of strategic objectives announced for the energy sector since the 1980s, there has been little evidence of either coherence of these objectives or of well-considered means by which these objectives could be achieved. . . .

By the late 1990s China had become a net importer of energy. The need for energy conservation and energy efficiency was re-emphasized and greater efforts were spent on developing indigenous energy resources, especially natural gas and hydroelectricity. A new theme was to encourage investment by national petroleum companies in overseas oil and gas reserves

The Costs of Meeting Energy Needs

The most immediate problem for China is that its economic growth is already outstripping its energy supplies. In boomtowns from Shenzhen to Chengdu, electricity is now an unstable commodity. [In 2004], 24 of China's 31 provinces, municipalities and autonomous regions admitted that they lacked sufficient power. In the summer, when drought curtails hydropower and air conditioners surge into life, blackouts have become commonplace.

The nation's coal mines are straining to meet the demand, at a terrible human cost. According to conservative official estimates, more than 6,000 workers were killed in China's mines [in 2004]—making them the world's most dangerous—and the death rate was undiminished in the first half of 2005.

Most coal-related fatalities never make the headlines, however. Many Chinese cities fail to meet international—or even their own—standards for air quality, causing hundreds of thousands of premature deaths each year. China's increasing use of coal is also sending CO_2 emissions skyrocketing, threatening a global climate disaster.

Peter Aldhous, Nature, *June 30, 2005.*

in the belief that access to such supplies would enhance the country's security of energy supply. As oil imports continued to increase, the high level of oil international prices forced the issue of strategic stockpiles onto the agenda in 2002.

The main energy challenge for the government during the 1980s and 1990s was to provide the nation with sufficient energy to sustain the extraordinary rate of economic growth. In this they were successful. Investment capacity to produce, transform and distribute energy allowed China's consumption of primary energy to double to 930 million tons of oil equivalent in 1996, just before the Asian financial crisis, from 470 million tons in 1983. The downside of this growth and the continued reliance on coal has been the ever increasing levels of atmospheric pollution at local, regional and global scales. To date the government has failed to integrate environmental concerns into its energy policy in a sustained and consistent manner. . . .

A major policy discontinuity exists between the government's desire to promote economic growth through infrastructure investment and rising consumer demand, on the one hand, and the way in which the energy sector is managed, on the other. While much of China's economy is operating in a relatively free, albeit distorted, market spurred on by government investment in infrastructure, the energy sector remains predominantly state-owned, and energy prices continue to be controlled by the state. As a result consumers are not receiving adequate signals to curb energy consumption and producers are not incentivized to invest in new capacity.

In 2003, the newly installed government realized that the country was facing an energy crisis and that the main threat to security of energy supply was domestic rather than international. A year later Beijing announced a new draft energy strategy which emphasized the overriding importance of energy efficiency and energy conservation and which set specific targets for energy savings. However the announcements lacked details on how such targets were to be met, and to date there is little sign of a truly new approach to energy policy.

These weaknesses in China's current energy policy can be traced primarily to the absence of an Energy Ministry or equivalent strong and well-staffed agency responsible for energy policy. The fragmented institutional structure of the energy industry has led to a fragmented energy policy, aggregated from specific industry objectives driven more by the leaders of these industries than by the formulation of sector-wide initiatives.

A Lack of Leadership

Until the mid-1990s China's energy sector was dominated by a small number of very large state-owned companies or ministries which fulfilled the functions of both enterprise and government. They reported to the State Planning Commission (SPC) and the State Economic and Trade Commission (SETC) which respectively held responsibility for strategic and operational matters. Most importantly the SPC was required to approve all major investments and all energy prices.

The year 1998 saw the start of a process of major restructuring of both government and large energy companies which marked an important step in the drive to corporatize and improve the performance of the sector. The key government functions relating to the energy sector were allocated to the renamed State Development Planning Commission (SDPC), the SETC and the newly created Ministry of Land and Resources. Clear strategic direction was lost as a result of these reforms, as the SDPC and SETC competed for leadership. This lack of clarity was resolved in 2003 when the SETC was abolished and the renamed National Development and Reform Commission (NDRC) took nominal control of energy strategy with the creation of an Energy Bureau. . . .

In the past, the leaders of the major state-owned energy companies were able to play a major role in determining the policies and plans for their individual industries. Progressive corporatization and disaggregation [breaking apart] of these companies has reduced the power of these executives to influence national policy to a great extent, but the capacity of government to lead has not been enhanced in a commensurate way. Indeed, with more players in the sector, the government's ability to manage the energy sector has actually diminished.

[The 2004] announcements on energy strategy and the recent formation of a leading group to oversee the energy sector clearly reflect a realization on the part of the most senior government officers that a new approach and a new institutional structure are required to address the short- and long-term challenges faced by China's energy sector. However, the creation of a leading group is an interim measure which should be followed by the establishment of a permanent agency at ministerial level, or above, with overall responsibility for energy. Such an agency will require a much higher level of staffing and of political authority than any of its predecessors, for radical measures will need to be taken along the entire energy supply chain. Of these measures, the most politically contentious will be the need for energy users to pay the full cost of their energy supply.

Future Steps

Assuming such a new energy agency is established, the future direction and nature of China's energy sector will depend on three further potential opportunities for change. The first will be a substantial improvement in the coherence of energy policy and in its linkage with environmental policy. Such a policy should not only state the objectives, but also the means through which these objectives will be achieved.

The second opportunity is for the government to undertake a radical change in their approach to the production, transformation and consumption of energy by bringing in measures and technologies to substantially enhance the efficiency and the cleanliness of the sector. The question is whether the future direction of energy strategy will be "business-as-usual" with incremental improvements at the margin, or a truly new approach.

Finally, and most importantly, Beijing needs to keep energy policy at or near the top of its agenda, and not allow it to be replaced by other pressing priorities once the crisis has passed. The energy sector in any country is highly politicized. If China's leaders really wish to change the way their energy is produced and used, then sustained political commitment will be required for many years.

"*The Chinese Medical Association now estimates that the cost of one average hospitalisation exceeds the average yearly income of 50% of the rural population.*"

China Faces a Health Crisis

Lancet

In the following viewpoint the Lancet, *a British health journal, argues that China's secrecy about epidemics and other health issues masks an outdated, underfunded, and failing public health system. According to the authors, contagious diseases such as SARS (severe acute respiratory syndrome) and AIDS spread rapidly in China because the health system was unprepared to deal with them. Because China's health system is not expected to improve anytime soon and few people can afford the exorbitant costs of hospital stays or doctors' visits, the* Lancet *maintains, many Chinese will die from common illnesses or diseases that should have been eradicated long ago.*

As you read, consider the following questions:

1. As the *Lancet* reports, by what percentage has infant mortality risen in China's western hinterlands in the new millennium?

The Lancet, "China Must Prioritise Health Opportunities for All," vol. 364, September 11, 2004, pp. 909–10. Copyright © 2004 by Elsevier Health Services. Reproduced by permission.

2. According to the authors, what did the reform-minded Chinese government hope would improve health care for the entire nation?

3. In the journal's view, on what has the aging Chinese population forced the health care system to focus? What, then, has been ignored because of this focus?

D enial, deception, and discrimination have characterised the AIDS epidemic in China. Since the first cases were identified in 1985, the Chinese Government has guarded infection rates as if they were state secrets. Groups at high risk of infection have been targeted for abuse by police, and whistleblowers bent on exposing the true extent of the epidemic have been harassed or even jailed.

[In September 2004], however, a law was passed that tackles some of the fundamental obstacles standing in the way of campaigns to halt HIV's spread. China's parliament, the National People's Congress, voted in favour of legislation to outlaw discrimination against people infected with a contagious disease and those suspected of harbouring infection. The new law also bans the buying and selling of blood—a trade that is thought to have spread infection to around 1 million farmers in China's Henan province during the 1990s—and stipulates that governments should strengthen prevention and control of AIDS.

This law is the first in which AIDS is specifically targeted. And although vague about how violations of the law will be monitored or punishments enforced, it proves that China is prepared to combat the epidemic through legal channels. By making such a statement, China has provided the international community with long-awaited confirmation that it now takes the threat of AIDS seriously. Unfortunately, however, sluggishness on this issue has allowed deep troubles in China's health system to go largely unnoticed.

A Nation Unprepared for Epidemics

International attention has generally focused on China's secrecy about health problems, diverting vital consideration away from the country's scandalous neglect of its rural health infrastructure, which is now starting to crumble. The outbreak of SARS [severe acute respiratory syndrome] in 2003 exposed the dilapidation of China's rural health-care facilities. Reports leaked to international media showed doctors in SARS-affected villages so poorly equipped that they lacked even sufficient numbers of surgical masks to protect medical staff. Among China's poorest communities, health indicators reveal the extent of neglect. In the western hinterlands, infant mortality has increased by 50% during recent years and nutrition statistics show continued decreases in health status.

These images contrast starkly with the population-wide figures that show consistent overall improvements in life expectancy and child mortality. In urban areas, along the eastern seaboard, the break-neck growth that characterised China's transition to a market-based economy is mirrored in the population's health. Large businesses have their own hospitals for treating employees, and government insurance schemes serve most of those with jobs. In rural areas, however, there are few businesses to foot the health-care bill. Cooperative schemes, the hallmark of China's pre-capitalist economy, were supposed to provide health for all—and did so during the 1970s. But since embracing market reform, China has persistently ignored rural health services, gambling instead on the promise that health improvements will accompany economic growth.

When the Maoist agricultural collectives began to disintegrate in the early 1980s, no replacements were proffered for the health services they supported. State investment in the health sector has halved during the past 20 years and hospitals, many of which remain state-owned, have been forced to make up their income by levying user fees that are prohibi-

Medical Costs Rise, Government Contributions Fall

According to Dr Rao [Kegin, director of the information centre at China's ministry of health], China's overall medical costs rose from 4.1 per cent of GDP [gross domestic product] to 5.3 per cent between 1991 and 2000, or from $11bn [billion] to $59.5bn. However, in the same period, the proportion of these overall medical costs that was contributed by the government dropped from 22.8 per cent to 14.9 per cent, while the share of individual spending rose from 38 per cent to 60.6 per cent. China's government spends less on health than most other developing countries.

Xiong Lei, New Statesman, *January 1, 2005.*

tively expensive for large swathes of the population. The Chinese Medical Association now estimates that the cost of one average hospitalisation exceeds the average yearly income of 50% of the rural population. China's economic success is certainly not rubbing off on its poor.

An Ageing Population and Recurring Ailments

Although classed as a middle-income country by the World Bank, China's disease profile is more similar to high-income countries than to others in its group. High average life expectancies mean that chronic diseases such as diabetes and cancer are common. And thanks to the infamous one-child [per married couple] policy, China is afflicted by another syndrome of development: an ageing population. This demographic profile has pushed health facilities to concentrate on chronic diseases, but worryingly this shift has sidelined services geared towards infection.

Whereas the potential explosion of China's AIDS problem is much discussed, less often mentioned is the resurgence of communicable diseases that were once considered under control. Infections such as tuberculosis and hepatitis B are rife in rural areas, and poverty has caused the migrant worker population to swell, providing a ready conduit for disease spread. Several recent epidemics have been traced back to infections transmitted by these mobile workers. China also has a policy of charging parents for childhood vaccinations; it is the only country in the world to do so and the consequences of such a strategy are disturbingly predictable.

After decades of neglect, China's health services are approaching a crisis. The population is unable to afford basic treatments and hospitals are unprepared for the most immediate threats. Yet the proportion of the country's GDP [gross domestic product] that is spent on health remains lower than that of similar-sized India—and most of this money comes straight from the pockets of patients. Some health reforms, at least, are underway. But the country-wide roll-out of experimental insurance systems for the very poor is not expected until 2010, by which time many will have died because they can't afford treatment.

China's internal problems are severe, but they are not just a domestic issue. The threat of uncontained disease poses a huge risk to the rest of the region, and perhaps the world. SARS has given us a glimpse of what could happen if an outbreak emerges in China's rural backwaters. It is in everyone's interest that China embraces change.

> "*Rising [state-society] tensions increase the risks that any reforms, even implemented as remedies, could trigger a revolution. . . . This sobering prospect could deter . . . the [Chinese Communist Party] from pursuing change.*"

China Faces a Governance Crisis

Minxin Pei

Since the Chinese Communist Party (CCP) declared its intent to institute democratic reforms in the 1980s, it has struggled to loosen its grip on the economy while maintaining its unchallenged authority over the nation. In the following viewpoint Minxin Pei argues that the CCP has fooled some Chinese and many foreigners into believing that China's booming economy is evidence of the government's progressive path. However, says Pei, this "dot communism"—one that bases its strength on economic growth rates—has failed to transfer power to the people and businesses that would ensure China's continued growth. Pei is currently a senior associate and director of the China Program of the Carnegie Endowment for International Peace.

As you read, consider the following questions:

1. According to Pei, what are four pathologies of a "degenerating governing capacity" that are evident in China?

Minxin Pei, "China's Governance Crisis," *Foreign Affairs*, vol. 81, September/October 2002, p. 96. Copyright © 2002 by the Council on Foreign Relations, Inc. Reproduced by permission.

2. What evidence does Pei give to suggest that the CCP cannot enforce internal discipline—especially in the troubling cases of corruption?

3. In the words of a Ministry of Public Security report, what was the only likely way in which the government could carry out tax collection and family planning policies in some parts of rural China?

The idea of an impending governance crisis in Beijing may sound unduly alarmist. To the outside world, China is a picture of dynamism and promise. . . . But beneath this giddy image of progress and prosperity lies a different reality—one that is concealed by the glitzy skylines of Shanghai, Beijing, and other coastal cities. The future of China, and the West's interests there, depends critically on how Beijing's new leaders deal with this somber reality.

Communism and Its Discontents

China's current crisis results from fundamental contradictions in the reforms that it has pursued over the past two decades—a period that has seen the amazing transformation of the communist regime from one that was infatuated with class struggle to one obsessed by growth rates. This "dot communism," characterized by the marriage of a Leninist party to bureaucratic capitalism with a globalist gloss, has merely disguised, rather than eliminated, these contradictions. But they are growing ever harder to ignore. The previously hidden costs of transition have begun to surface: Further change implies not simply a deepening of market liberalization but also the implementation of political reforms that could endanger the CCP's [Chinese Communist Party's] monopoly on power.

These emerging contradictions are embedded in the very nature of the Chinese regime. For example, the government's market-oriented economic policies, pursued in a context of autocratic and predatory politics, make the CCP look like a self-serving, capitalistic ruling elite, and not a "proletarian party" championing the interests of working people. The party's professed determination to maintain political supremacy also runs counter to its declared goals of developing a "socialist market economy" and "ruling the country according to law," because the minimum requirements of a market economy and the rule of law are institutionalized curbs on political power. The CCP's ambition to modernize Chinese society leaves unanswered the question of how increasing social autonomy will be protected from government caprice. And the party's perennial fear of independently organized interest groups does not prepare it for the inevitable emergence of such groups in an industrialized economy. These unresolved contradictions, inherent in the country's transition away from communism, are the source of rising tensions in China's polity, economy, and society.

During the go-go 1990s, the irreconcilable nature of these contradictions was obscured by rising prosperity and relative political tranquility. Economically, accelerating liberalization and deepening integration with the world marketplace produced unprecedented prosperity, even though some tough reforms (especially those affecting the financial sector and state-owned enterprises, or SOEs) lagged behind. Politically, the ruling elite drew its own lesson from the collapse of Soviet communism ("It's the economy, stupid") and closed ranks behind a strategy that prioritized economic growth and left the political system untouched. . . .

The incompatibilities between China's current political system, however, and the essential requirements of the rule of law, a market economy, and an open society have not been washed away by waves of foreign investment. Pragmatists might view these contradictions as inconsequential cognitive nuisances. Unfortunately, their effects are real: they foreclose reform options that otherwise could be adopted for the regime's own long-term good. To be sure, China's pragmatic leaders have made a series of tactical adjustments to weather many new socioeconomic challenges, such as the CCP's recent outreach to entrepreneurs. But these moves are no substitute for genuine institutional reforms that would reinvigorate and relegitimize the ruling party.

In retrospect, the 1990s ought to be viewed as a decade of missed opportunities. The CCP leadership could have taken advantage of a booming economy to renew itself through a program of gradual political reform built on the rudimentary steps of the 1980s. But it did not, and now the cumulative costs of a decade of foot-dragging are becoming more visible. . . .

These pathologies—such as pervasive corruption, a collusive local officialdom, elite cynicism, and mass disenchantment—are the classic symptoms of degenerating governing capacity. . . . In a Leninist party-state however, effective governance critically hinges on the health of the ruling party. Strong organizational discipline, accountability, and a set of core values with broad appeal are essential to governing effectively. Deterioration of the ruling party's strength, on the other hand, sets in motion a downward cycle that can severely impair the party-state's capacity to govern.

Numerous signs within China indicate that precisely such a process is producing huge governance deficits. The resulting strains are making the political and economic choices of China's rulers increasingly untenable. They may soon be forced to undertake risky reforms to stop the rot. If they do not, dot communism could be no more durable than the dot coms. . . .

The Decline of the Communist Party

The extent of the CCP's decline can be measured in three areas: the shrinkage of its organizational penetration, the erosion of its authority and appeal among the masses, and the breakdown of its internal discipline. The organizational de-

Lane. © 2002 by Cagle Cartoons, Inc. Reproduced by permission.

cline of the CCP is, in retrospect, almost predetermined. Historically, Leninist parties have thrived only in economies dominated by the state. . . . By pursuing market reforms that have eliminated rural communes and most SOEs, the CCP has fallen victim to its own success. The new economic infrastructure, based on household farming, private business, and individual labor mobility, is inhospitable to a large party apparatus. . . . In 2000, the CCP did not have a single member in 86 percent of the country's 1.5 million private firms and could establish cells in only one percent of private companies.

The CCP's organizational decay is paralleled by the decline of its authority and image among the public. A survey of 818 migrant laborers in Beijing in 1997–98 revealed that the prevailing image of the ruling party was that of a self-serving elite. Only 5 percent of the interviewees thought their local party cadres "work for the interests of the villagers," and 60 percent said their local officials "use their power only for private gains." Other surveys have revealed similar negative public perceptions of the CCP. . . .

At the same time as public officials are losing respect, the party's ideological appeal has all but evaporated. . . . Even members of the ruling elite are beginning, albeit reluctantly, to admit this reality. . . .

At the heart of the CCP's organizational and reputational decline is the breakdown of its members' ideological beliefs and internal discipline. Cynicism and corruption abound. . . .

Even more worrying, the CCP appears unable to enforce internal discipline despite the mortal threat posed by corruption, which has surpassed unemployment as the most serious cause of social instability. Recent official actions, especially the prosecution and execution of several senior officials, create the impression that the CCP leadership is committed to combating corruption. But a comprehensive look at the data tells a different story. Most corrupt officials caught in the government's dragnet seem to have gotten off with no more than a slap on the wrist. . . . According to a top CCP official, the party has in recent years expelled only about one percent of its members.

Perhaps the greatest contributing factor to the CCP's political decline is, ironically, the absence of competition. Competition would have forced the party to redefine its mission and recruit members with genuine public appeal. But like monopoly firms, the CCP has devoted its energies to preventing the emergence of competition. Without external pressures, monopolies such as the CCP inevitably develop a full range of pathologies such as patronage systems, organizational dystrophy, and unresponsiveness. Moreover, one-party regimes can rarely take on the new competitors that emerge when the political environment changes suddenly. The fall of the Soviet bloc regimes and the defeat of similar monopolistic parties in the developing world . . . show that an eroding capacity for political mobilization poses a long-term threat to the CCP.

The State Fails Its People

In a party-state, the ruling party's weakness unavoidably saps the state's power. Such "state incapacitation," which in its extreme form results in failed states, is exemplified by the government's increasing inability to provide essential services, such as public safety, education, basic health care, environmental protection, and law enforcement. In China, these indices have been slipping over the past two decades. This decline is especially alarming since it has occurred while the Chinese economy has been booming. . . .

The central cause of the declining effectiveness of the Chinese state is a dysfunctional fiscal system that has severely undercut the government's ability to fund public services while creating ample opportunities for corruption. . . .

An important consequence of this dysfunctional fiscal system is the near collapse of local public finance in many counties and townships, particularly in the populous rural interior provinces (such as Henan, Anhui, and Hunan). . . .

The responsibilities of providing public services while supporting a bloated bureaucracy have forced many township governments deeply into debt.

In most counties, the state's declining fiscal health portends more serious maladies. The problems of the rural provinces should serve as an urgent warning to Beijing because these are historically the most unstable regions in the country, having previously generated large-scale peasant rebellions. Indeed, it is no coincidence that these agrarian provinces (where per capita income in 2000 was about half the national average) have in recent years seen the largest increase in peasant riots and tax revolts. . . .

The institutional decline of the ruling party and the weakness of the state have caused rising tensions between the state and society. The number of protests, riots, and other forms of resistance against state authorities has risen sharply. . . .

To be sure, rising social frustration results partly from the hardships produced by China's economic transition. In recent years, falling income in rural areas and growing unemployment in the cities have contributed to the rising discontent among tens of millions of peasants and workers. But the increasing frequency, scale, and intensity of collective defiance and individual resistance also reveal deep flaws in Chinese political institutions that have exacerbated the strains of transition. Social frustration is translated into political protest not merely because of economic deprivation, but because of a growing sense of political injustice. Government officials who abuse their power and perpetrate acts of petty despotism create resentment among ordinary citizens every day. These private grievances are more likely to find violent expression when the institutional mechanisms for resolving them (such as the courts, the press, and government bureaucracies) are inaccessible, unresponsive, and inadequate.

In rural China, where institutional rot is much more advanced, the tensions between the state and the peasantry have reached dangerous levels. In a startling internal report, the Ministry of Public Security admitted that "in some [rural] areas, enforcement of family-planning policy and collection of taxes would be impossible without the use of police force." In some villages, peasant resistance has grown so fierce that local officials dare not show their faces; these areas have effectively became lawless.

The most important source of this anger is the onerous tax burden levied on China's most improverished citizens. . . . The combination of high payment, heavy-handed collection, and inadequate services has thus turned a large portion of the rural population against the state. Recent polls conducted in rural areas found that peasants consistently identify excessive taxes and fees as the most important cause of instability.

Significantly, relations between the state and society are growing more tense at a time of rising income inequality. . . . Recent surveys have found that inequality has become one of the top three concerns for the public. In the context of rampant official corruption, this rising inequality is likely to fuel public ire against the government because most people believe that only the corrupt and privileged can accumulate wealth. . . .

The absence of pressure valves within the Chinese political system will hamper the regime's ability to reduce and manage state-society tensions. Recent reforms, such as instituting village elections and improving the legal system, have proved inadequate. The CCP's failure to open up the political system and expand institutional channels for conflict resolution creates an environment in which aggrieved groups turn to collective protest to express frustrations and seek redress.

The accumulation of state-society tensions will eventually destabilize China, especially because the dynamics that generate such tensions trap the CCP in a hopeless dilemma. Rising tensions increase the risks that any reforms, even implemented as remedies, could trigger a revolution. [Nineteenth-century French political observer] Alexis de Tocqueville first observed this paradox: repressive regimes are most likely to be overthrown when they try to reform themselves. This sobering prospect could deter even the most progressive elements within the CCP from pursuing change.

The Threat Continues

Remedying China's mounting governance deficits should be the top priority of the country's new leaders. At present, these problems, brought on by the contradictions of dot communism, are serious but not life-threatening. If the new leadership addresses the institutional sources of poor governance, the CCP may be able to manage its problems without risking a political upheaval. The unfolding succession drama, however, will get in the way of meaningful change in the short term. Proposing even a moderate reform program could jeopardize a leader's political prospects. Moreover, undertaking risky reforms would require a high level of party unity—unlikely from a leadership jockeying for power.

Thus, China's governance deficits are likely to continue to grow and threaten the sustainability of its economic development. The slow-brewing crisis of governance may not cause an imminent collapse of the regime, but the accumulation of severe strains on the political system will eventually weigh down China's economic modernization as poor governance makes trade and investment more costly and more risky. The current economic dynamism may soon fade as long-term stagnation sets in.

Periodical Bibliography

The following articles have been selected to supplement the diverse views presented in this chapter.

Hannah Beech	"China's Baby Bust: A Dwindling Birthrate and an Aging Populace Force China to Rethink Its Family-Planning Policy," *Time International,* July 31, 2001.
Brian Bremer and John Carey	"Wasteful Ways: Colossally Inefficient Use of Energy Penalizes China Twice: With High Costs and the Ravages of Pollution," *Business Week,* April 11, 2005.
Economist	"Gate-Crashing the Party: Politics in China," November 15, 2003.
Bates Gill, Jennifer Chang, and Sarah Palmer	"China's HIV Crisis," *Foreign Affairs,* March/April 2002.
Ken Kostel	"China Promises Pollution Cleanup," *Discover,* January 2005.
David D. Li and Ling Li	"A Simple Solution to China's Pension Crisis," *Cato Journal,* Fall 2003.
Jianguo Liu and Jared Diamond	"China's Environment in a Globalizing World," *Nature,* June 30, 2005.
Anne Loussouarn	"Pollution Poisons China's Progress," *USA Today,* July 5, 2005.
Roderick Macfarquhar	"Unhealthy Politics: China's Leaders' Response to SARS," *Newsweek International,* May 12, 2003.
Dexter Roberts	"A Safety Net That's Barely There," *Business Week,* January 31, 2005.
Jonathan Watts	"Rich Tomorrow, Maybe, but Filthy Today," *New Statesman,* January 1, 2005.
World & I	"The Specter of SARS: China's Failure to Contain Severe Acute Respiratory Syndrome Has Economic Causes and Consequences," July 2003.

How Strong Is China's Economy?

Chapter Preface

Only within the last seventy years has China's economy switched from primarily agrarian to one that is focused on industry and technology. The shift has been monumental in scope and has been aided since the 1980s by economic reforms designed to open China's markets to global trade. These reforms have permitted limited private enterprise to take hold in a nation that has traditionally favored state-owned industry. To be sure, state-owned operations are still the norm—and corruption and bureaucracy still plague that sector—but China's ministers are experimenting with what they believe to be the favorable elements of capitalism to promote growth and reduce poverty. This experiment is a remarkable sea change for a nation that prided itself as the antithesis of Western ideology. Indeed, as Princeton professor of political economy Gregory C. Chow states, the current embrace of capitalism left Communist ideals high and dry, and "the slogans condemning the evil of capitalism were changed to 'getting rich is glorious.'"

In its pursuit of wealth, the new "capitalist" economy of China has been growing by around 8 percent per year since 1998, and export volume has increased. China also joined the World Trade Organization in 2001, so its exports have been flooding numerous world markets, and foreign capital has come streaming to the mainland. Chow suggests that by 2020, China's production output could match that of the United States. For the Chinese the benefits have translated into higher incomes and improved standards of living for a rising middle class. Some in America see China's rapid economic growth less favorably. Many analysts and commentators fear that U.S. industry will not be able to compete with China's inexhaustible manpower and the relatively low production costs of merchandise. They also fear that American workers will suffer as U.S. corporations flee to China to take advantage of the inexpensive labor.

In the following chapter Robert E. Scott and Stephen Roach debate the issue of whether China's economic growth will have negative consequences for the United States. Other articles in the chapter examine the strengths and weaknesses of the Chinese economy and likewise try to predict the future of the new, "capitalist" China.

> *"China [has] much more internal dynamics to sustain . . . [a] longer period of high growth, . . . and it will take many decades before China exhausts its total development potential."*

China Can Sustain Economic Growth

John Wong and Sarah Chan

In the following viewpoint John Wong and Sarah Chan, associates of the National University of Singapore, contend that China's economic development will continue unabated as long as China remains committed to progress. The nation, Wong and Chan argue, has yet to tap its true resource potential, and the authors dispute claims that positive forecasts of China's economic growth are based on flawed interpretations of the evidence. China's economy, they maintain, is buoyed by internal demand and growth, not by exports. Indeed, if exports were slowed by tariffs or other limitations, the authors claim, China's economic growth would continue.

As you read, consider the following questions:

1. How do Wong and Chan refute Thomas Rawski's claim

John Wong and Sarah Chan, "Why China's Economy Can Sustain High Performance: An Analysis of Its Sources of Growth," *The Royal Institute of International Affairs, Asia Programme Working Paper,* July 2003, p. 1,608. Copyright © 2003 by John Wong and Sarah Chan. All rights reserved. Reproduced by permission.

that China's industry was slowing because the nation's energy consumption was declining?

2. What percent of China's continued economic growth was driven by internal demand for products and services in the first three quarters of 2002, according to the authors?

3. What, according to Wong and Chan, is China's rank among the largest exporting nations in the world?

The Chinese economy has experienced spectacular growth, averaging 9.5% a year since 1978. The 1997 Asian financial crisis brought down many Asian economies but China's economy was hardly affected, and it continued to grow at 8.8% in 1997 and 7.8% in 1998.

More recently, while economic growth in most of Asia has been plummeting to low or negative growth as the world economy at large is creeping into recession, China's economy alone is still steaming ahead with strong growth. In 2002, China's economy expanded by a robust 8%, amidst the general gloom and doom in market sentiment in the region....

Refuting Western Interpretations

A number of Western journalists and scholars have taken issue with Chinese official statistics for their gross inaccuracy which greatly exaggerated China's economic performance. The controversy was rekindled by a study [published in 2001] by American scholar Thomas Rawski, who observed that official growth figures for China's GDP [gross domestic product] and industrial production do not reconcile with lower growth rates for other indicators such as energy use. Rawski noted that increases in China's GDP and industrial production since 1998 were negatively correlated with a decline in energy consumption. China's actual GDP growth could range from negative growth in 1998 and 1999, to 2–3 percent in 2000—a far cry from the official growth figures of 7–8 percent. Rawski's argument was soon widely picked up by Western media due to its sensational nature.

A number of Chinese scholars and statisticians have since refuted Rawski's argument for being "groundless". They cogently argue that with the growth of the service sector in China and the shift of its industrial structure from smoke-stacked heavy industries to light and high-tech industries, it would be unrealistic for Rawski to expect any close correlation between growth in industrial production and growth in energy consumption. In most industrial countries, economic growth is actually accompanied by a decline in energy consumption. In China, its new growth industries in recent years are the light and high-tech industries such as electronics and electrical machinery which are not energy intensive. There should therefore be no permanent causal relationship between GDP growth and energy consumption.

Some scholars have also refuted Rawski's claim that Chinese official growth statistics are highly questionable. Economics Nobel Laureate Lawrence Klein and his associate, employing a more comprehensive test of the relations between China's GDP and 15 other major indicators (not just energy but also electricity, grain, steel, freight, civil aviation, long-distance phone and so on) for the whole period of 1980–2000, confirm that the movements of these major economic components "are consistent with the movements of real GDP as officially estimated". Klein has qualified that their study has not "proved" that Chinese official GDP measure is correct; as no one knows the "correct estimate".

Another noted American economist Nicholas Lardy pointed to a few indicators that supported Chinese official growth data. First, China's import growth of 70% between 1997 and 2001 does not support the contention that the economy is contracting nor sharply decelerating. The most plausible explanation for the high import growth figures, consistent with export data in trading partner countries, is an ex-

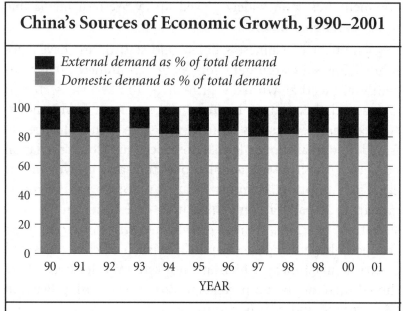

China's Sources of Economic Growth, 1990–2001

■ *External demand as % of total demand*
■ *Domestic demand as % of total demand*

YEAR

Total demand comprises domestic demand (i.e., consumption and investment of both private and public sectors, plus changes in inventories) and external demand (i.e. exports).

Computed from data in *China Statistical Yearbook* (relevant years), published by the Economist Intelligence Unit.

pansion of GDP. Modest tariff reductions are unlikely to explain more than a fifth of the growth of imports. Second, family incomes and household savings have been steadily rising, which is a sign of a growing, not faltering economy....

Another Asian Success Story

In fact, seen in the historical context of many high-performance East Asian economies, China's high economic growth for the past two decades as reflected in its official GDP statistics, though very impressive, is actually not exceptional. China's growth rates are comparable to the phenomenal growth rates of Japan and the other East Asian countries. Japan experienced near double-digit rates of growth in the 1950s, 1960s and most of the 1970s, while the newly-industrialised economies of South Korea, Taiwan, Hong Kong and Singapore, experienced growth for more than three decades from the 1960s to the 1980s. Several ASEAN [Association of Southeast Asian Nations, an economic-growth organization] countries like Malaysia, Indonesia and Thailand also experienced similar high growth performance in the 1970s and 1980s.

China is a much larger country than its East Asian neighbours. China [has] much more internal dynamics to sustain an even longer period of high growth, as it has virtually a whole continent to develop and it will take many decades before China exhausts its total development potential. Empirically speaking, the sceptical views of China's economy are just not consistent with the historical experiences of the East Asian economies.

Domestic Demand as a Major Driving Force

How do we explain China's dynamic economic growth? For a huge continental economy like China, domestic demand naturally constitutes the mainstay of its economic growth. As shown in Figure 1, domestic demand was responsible for over 90% of China's total demand in the early and mid-1980s. In recent years, as China's exports continued to surge, domestic demand still stood at about 80%. This proportion is about the exact opposite of that for the highly open Singapore and Hong Kong economies, with their growth depending predominantly on external demand. In fact, China's 7.9% growth in the first three quarters of 2002 was basically fuelled by domestic investment, which actually increased 21.8% over the same period. This explains why China's economy can continue to grow at high rates quite independent of the ebbs and flows of the international economy.

From a demand perspective, China's high growth stems from its high levels of domestic investment, being matched by equally high levels of domestic savings which were over 30% of GDP in the 1980s and above 40% in the 1990s. Accordingly, the Chinese government was able to mobilise such [a] huge pool of savings for infrastructural investment, and this easily translates into high GDP growth. . . .

How have domestic consumption *C* and domestic investment *I* actually contributed to growth over the past two decades? Table 1 gives a break-down of China's sources of growth for the whole period. It can be seen that household and government consumption has been the major source of growth for most years except for the boom years of 1985 and 1993, when domestic investment took over as the main driver of growth. This means the economy got overheated when China was over-investing. At the same time, the proportions of exports, whilst fluctuating widely, made only a marginal contribution to growth except for two or three years. . . .

Exports Rising

Is the contribution of external demand to China's economic growth of only marginal significance? What has happened to China's open-door policy? By conventional measure, the Chinese economy today is quite "open" as reflected by its trade-GDP ratio which rose from 15% in 1982 to 48% in 2000. In fact, on the basis of export-GDP ratio, China can be ranked economically more open than [the] USA and Japan! This is because China's nominal GDP tends to be downward-biased on account of its old socialist pricing structures whereas exports are denominated in US dollar terms. . . .

It makes sense to say that China is economically less open than Japan and USA, and very much so compared to the four East Asian NIEs [newly industrialized economies, such as Hong Kong, Singapore, Taiwan, and South Korea] and ASEAN-4 [Indonesia, Malaysia, Philippines, and Thailand]. . . . A large economy, be it Japan, USA or China, tends to be more self-sufficient and therefore less dependent on trade. . . .

It may be stressed that though China's exports (at US$266 billion in 2001) may be nominally very large in absolute terms, making it the world's sixth largest exporting nation, the net-value-added of its export trade remains relatively low. First, almost 50% of China's exports are generated by foreign enterprises. Second and more importantly, China's exports are heavily dependent on the import of intermediate products, estimated to be as high as 50%. As the domestic content of China's exports is low, its domestic value-added or contribution to GDP will necessarily remain low. Hence the small contribution of external demand to China's GDP growth.

Viewed from a different angle, however, China's exports are economically not all that unimportant, even if we take into account its relatively low domestic content. It is commonly acknowledged that China's export sector is the single most vibrant segment of the whole economy because of its better management and better technology. As such, it must have exerted a strong catalytic effect on the rest of the economy, creating a much greater total linkage effect than what is shown in our foregoing analysis. In other words, our limited exercise here has probably failed to capture all the "spread effects" of the export sector. A proper approach would need to trace all the multiplier effects of the foreign trade sector through a detailed input-output table.

Of even greater importance, our analysis has shown that even though the share of export's contribution to GDP is still very small, it is clearly rising. . . . China's WTO [World Trade Organization] membership will certainly accelerate this rising trend.

An Optimistic Forecast

To conclude, China as a large continental sized economy will continue to depend primarily on its internal dynamics for its long-term growth. The contribution of external demand to growth will nominally remain small. But external demand is

clearly rising, and it is set to play a more important supporting role for China's future economic growth, particularly when
domestic demand falters. Since the 1997 Asian financial crisis,
the Chinese government has come to rely on increasing fixed
investment to pump prime growth. Beijing cannot continue
with this proactive fiscal policy for long without running into
unacceptable levels of fiscal deficits. External demand will
have to come in to play an increasingly crucial role in supporting China's future economic growth.

> *"China's economy has grown quickly but unevenly, unsustainably, and even dangerously."*

China Cannot Sustain Economic Growth

Bruce Gilley

In the following viewpoint Bruce Gilley argues that China will not be able to sustain its economic growth if its government refuses to open the nation up to democratic reforms. According to Gilley, the government's economic policies are hampering continued growth by fostering corruption, tax evasion, and fraud, leaving the populace with no confidence in the system. Without opening the country to democracy and thus encouraging private enterprise and free trade, Gilley claims, China's economy will slow. Bruce Gilley, a former contributing editor to the Far Eastern Economic Review, *is the author of* China's Democratic Future: How It Will Happen and Where It Will Lead, *from which this viewpoint is excerpted.*

As you read, consider the following questions:

1. According to Gilley, what did 82 percent of the engineering, computer science, and physics students do after graduating from Qinghua University in 2001?

2. From statistics provided by China's central government and cited by the author, what percentage of private businesses fail to pay taxes in China?

3. In Gilley's opinion, how much capital is leaving China every year because the business community and the public at large have no confidence in the nation's fiscal policies?

Assume that all the injustice, inequality, waste, costs, and pure heartbreak of the marketization of China's economy between 1978 and the end of the twentieth century was somehow worthwhile. A bigger question is whether the same program is sustainable in the first decades of the twenty-first century. If the argument for democracy was not compelling at first, it is certainly compelling now. For the same democracy deficit that hampered and misdirected the gains of the first two decades of reform [under Deng Xiaoping from the late 1970s through the late 1990s] is now preventing China from creating sustainable growth for the coming decades. Note two scholars in China [Zhang Lei and Cheng Linsheng in a 1999 book]: "The biggest advocates of political reforms today are not academics and intellectuals but economists and businessmen who appreciate most keenly the need for political reforms to keep up with reforms in their areas."

A Need for Innovation and Political Reform

Here we consider five aspects of sustainability: innovation, effective regulation, safety, environmental protection, and financial health.

Gains from reallocations of labor and capital out of industry [into light industry, technology, and private enterprise] are likely to dry up as a source of growth by 2015, according to the World Bank. The gains from marketization will also end sometime in the first decade of the century. Already, growth is more and more dependent on fiscal stimulus, without which, the premier Zhu Rongji said in early 2002, the economy "might have collapsed." That means China's economy will have to rely more and more on technical improvements to grow. As is well known, innovation thrives under democracy. It requires open information sources, free debate, guaranteed rights, and secure contracts—of the sort that only democracy has proven consistently able to deliver. The necessity of democracy to spur technological change was noted in a famous speech by liberal Party elder Wan Li in 1986. A prominent scholar of the Central Party School repeated the call a decade later: "The serious lagging of political reform is now a major obstacle to sustainable economic growth."

Yet at present, China's technical innovation capacity is woefully low. Its best scientists and entrepreneurs go abroad—82 percent of engineering, computer science, and physics graduates from Qinghua University left the country in 2001—or register their companies abroad, because of the uncertainties of pursuing their vocations in China. Its home-grown companies, nurtured on clientelist ties to the state, find they cannot compete in world markets. All that creates a pressing demand in society for the openness and security of democracy. As one [Chinese] economist wrote in a [2000] state report: "There is not a single successful market economy in the world that is not also a democracy."

Ineffective Regulation

Closely tied to innovation is the need for effective regulation. Here, reform China may have created one of the world's most badly regulated economies. Smuggling, counterfeiting, fraud, extortion, tax evasion, gangsters, and cronyism thrive on a scale never before seen. Half of the four billion contracts signed every year are fraudulent in some respect, according to official estimates. An estimated 40 percent of all products

The Toll of Unemployment on China's Economy

Open and disguised unemployment in China amounts to about 170 million, or 23 percent of the total labor force. Recent and prospective increases in unemployment have been principally due to population increases in the 1980s, and the privatization and downsizing of the often inefficient, loss incurring state-owned enterprises. China's efforts to comply with its World Trade Organization (WTO) commitments may engender more unemployment. Rural poverty has led to increased income inequality between rural and urban areas, rural-to-urban migration, rising urban unemployment, and social unrest.

Potential worsening of these adversities may cause a reduction between 0.3 and 0.8 percent in China's annual growth rate in the coming decade, as a result of lower factor productivity, lower savings, and reduced capital formation.

Charles Wolf Jr., Asia Program Special Report, June 2003.

made in the country are either fake or substandard. The central government estimates that 80 percent of private entrepreneurs avoid taxes in some way. Meanwhile, two-thirds of the biggest 1,300 state enterprises keep false accounts.

The costs of this are real. Credit cards, checks, and e-commerce cannot develop. People die from fake booze. A black market in human organs thrives. Long-term private investment is stifled. Critical public investments in research, social welfare, education, and health are impossible. Public assets are privatized, plundered, and left to rot. Growth becomes almost impossible. Without free newspapers or opposition parties, the control of wrongdoing becomes stalled by closed political networks. The argument for CCP [Chinese Communist Party]-style reforms, wrote three U.S. economists [Jeffrey D. Sachs, Wing Thye Woo, and Xiaokai Yang in 2000], "may be overlooking the social tensions being created by the asset-stripping, corruption and macroeconomic instability" which "may cause a popular rebellion against the regime."

A strong central state could, in theory, impose order and regulations to create the "economic society" necessary for a properly functioning market economy, as Chile did in the 1970s. But in China, the decentralization of power that accompanied reforms and the rise of crony business networks both mean central edicts are a weak tool. Indeed, it is the state itself that is involved in most of the malfeasance. The only way to create the "economic society" of markets and rule of law is to limit political power. One Beijing scholar [Xie Qingkui] notes that the argument that dictatorship would spur growth by reducing the "transaction costs" of democracy has been turned on its head by the reality of widespread scams and inefficiencies bred by the closed political system. "The price we have paid is considerable, even massive. This is why it is urgent to begin democratic political reforms."

Safety and Environmental Issues Take Their Toll

Safety problems also stem from the lack of political oversight. Road safety is a good barometer of a state's ability to regulate a growing society. China's annual road carnage was 106,000 people in 2001, making it the world's most dangerous place to be in a vehicle, measured by deaths per vehicle on the road, and twice as deadly as in 1985. A person is 30 times more likely to die when getting into a vehicle in China than in the United States. Other types of accident are no less frequent: workplace accidents—everything from factory fires to flooded mine shafts to firecracker explosions—took another 25,000 lives in 2001. One mainland writer [Wang Jianqin] compares the response to accidents with that in newly democratic South Korea. "When a bridge collapsed in Seoul in 1995, the mayor resigned and seven city officials were arrested. But in China we have a daily parade of major accidents and the only thing that happens is that the relevant officials are praised for their work in the relief effort."

Ineffective regulation is perhaps seen most starkly in environmental degradation. Official and unofficial estimates put the annual losses due to pollution (both direct costs to agriculture and industry and indirect costs to health and buildings) at the equivalent of 4 to 8 percent of GDP [gross domestic product]. In addition, ecological damage (deforestation etc) is estimated variously at another 5 to 15 percent of GDP per year. This means that the economic value of China's natural assets is being reduced in a way that will constrain long-term growth.

There is also a cultural capital degradation that is harder to estimate. UNESCO [United Nations Education, Scientific, and Cultural Organization] officials constantly decry the degradation of the country's great cultural sites. Soaring new hotels have marred the riverside scenes of once-idyllic Guilin, while waves from tourist boats have eaten away at the river's Buddhist carvings. Cable cars have covered the country's once-sacred mountaintops.

This environmental disaster was not a necessary accompaniment to economic growth but an avoidable result of a lack of political pressure and open society. One farmer in Inner Mongolia who tried to prevent the illegal logging of hillsides near his home was arrested after he found evidence implicating local officials in the problem. . . . Saving China's environment, according to the World Bank, requires "a significant change in development strategy" that includes "public participation in environmental decision-making."

Flawed Financial Policies

Finally, the financial crisis bred by Beijing's flawed state enterprise reform strategy increasingly constrains growth prospects. By allowing corruption to steal away the best parts of the state sector, Beijing is left controlling the dregs. The state's big four banks are politically mandated to lend to these losers irrespective of performance. The result is a banking system where perhaps half of all loans are never going to be repaid. To keep savings flowing into state banks, the government mandates low interest rates and limits the activities of private and foreign banks (something unlikely to change despite WTO [World Trade Organization] promises).

Public confidence in state banks is weak. One result is capital flight. Estimates vary but a safe middle ground is that around $25 billion was leaving China every year at the turn of the century, most of it never to return. Another result is that finance is pushed underground. As much as half of all the money in the country's stock markets, a total of $100 billion, comes from illegal investment schemes. The state's use of the 1,300 listed companies as vehicles for the enrichment of local cadres causes wild swings in official policy. It also creates dangerously unstable fiscal conditions. The amount of outstanding public debt as a percentage of GDP exceeds 100 percent if pension and implicit guarantees to the banking sector are included.

Internationally, the pressures for a better financial system are immense. Analysts expect the Renminbi to become the world's fourth most heavily traded currency once it is convertible, expected around 2010. As the steward of one of the world's major currencies, Beijing will need a predictable and open monetary policy-setting apparatus. Yet the current system fails to deliver that because financial policy is driven by the changing imperatives of sustaining Party rule.

Overall, the picture is of an economy that could profit from a heavy dose of democracy. China's economy has grown quickly but unevenly, unsustainably, and even dangerously. Crisis looms on many fronts, from peasants to pensioners, from bad loans to bad products. What might have been a South Korean or Taiwanese style emergence into a relatively equal and robust market economy has instead become a Latin American-style land of corruption and inequality. "In delaying the introduction of democratic reforms," notes one Chinese scholar [Feng Chongyi], "the Chinese have missed the best chance to provide an equal start for everyone in the market-place."

It's never too late to curtail the losses of course. Many scholars in China now hearken back to [former Chinese leader] Deng Xiaoping's words that political reforms are the real marker of economic success. "If the top priority of China's rulers really were stability through the difficult times of re-maining economic reforms," concludes one Western scholar [Edward Friedman], "then they would already be working as-siduously to democratize China."

> "Growing trade deficits with China
> have displaced production supporting
> 1.5 million U.S. jobs since 1989."

China's Trade Policies Harm the U.S. Economy

Robert E. Scott

Robert E. Scott, director of international programs at the Economics Policy Institute (EPI), a nonpartisan research organization, argues in the following viewpoint that since 1989 many U.S. industries have been losing jobs and shipping their production departments overseas, often to China. Furthermore, Scott argues, while China's entry into the World Trade Organization (WTO) in 2001 was supposed to open up other world markets to Chinese goods and thus ease the burden on the United States, the fact remains that America is still China's largest trade partner and therefore suffers the most from the trade imbalance between the two countries.

As you read, consider the following questions:

1. According to statistics provided by Scott, how much did the U.S. trade deficit (with China) increase per year on average in 2002 and 2003?
2. In Scott's view, what did the U.S. motor vehicle and

Robert E. Scott, "U.S.-China Trade, 1989–2003: Impact on Jobs and Industries, Nationally and State-by-State," Economic Policy Institute, January 2005. www.epi.org. Reproduced by permission.

aerospace industries expect would happen when China joined the WTO? What really happened?

3. How have multinational firms working in China used WTO protections to their advantage, in the author's opinion?

The rise in the United States' trade deficit with China between 1989 and 2003 caused the displacement of production that supported 1.5 million U.S. jobs. Some of those jobs were related to production or services that ceased or moved elsewhere; others are jobs in supplying industries. These jobs reflect the effect on labor demand—in lost job opportunities—in an economy with a worsening balance between exports and imports. Most of those lost opportunities were in the high-wage and job-hemorrhaging manufacturing sector. The number of job opportunities lost each year grew rapidly during the 1990s, and accelerated after China entered the World Trade Organization (WTO) in 2001. The loss of these potential jobs is just the most visible tip of China's impact on the U.S. economy. . . .

The Growth of the Trade Deficit

The rate of growth of U.S. trade with China has accelerated since 1989, as shown in Figure 1. Between 1989 and 1997, U.S. imports from China grew an average of $6.4 billion per year; while exports increased about $1 billion per year. Thus the trade deficit widened $5.5 billion per year, on average, in this period.

Between 1997 and 2001, import growth increased more than 50% (to $10 billion per year) export growth picked up slightly (to $1.4 billion), and the trade gap expanded by $8.6 billion per year. Between 2001 and 2003, import growth jumped to $25 billion per year, a 150% rise in only four years. Exports grew rapidly, but not enough to offset the explosion in imports, so deficits increased, on average, $21 billion per year in 2002 and 2003, and these figures were restrained by the 2001 recession. The effect on the U.S. economy from trade trends with China has clearly jumped onto a different plane. . . .

Between 1989 and 2003, the growth in U.S. exports to China created demand that supported 199,000 additional U.S. jobs. In the same period, the growth of imports displaced production that could have supported an additional 1,659,000 jobs. As a result, growth in the U.S. trade with China eliminated a net 1,460,000 domestic job opportunities in this period. . . .

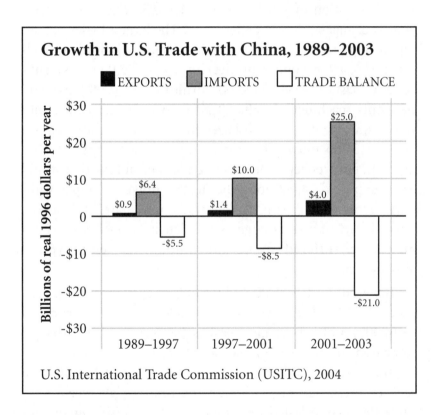

Growth in U.S. Trade with China, 1989–2003

■ EXPORTS ■ IMPORTS □ TRADE BALANCE

U.S. International Trade Commission (USITC), 2004

Some economists reject the general notion that growing trade deficits can cause a net loss of job opportunities. Their most common argument is that employment levels are determined by macroeconomic policies such as monetary and fiscal policies and, most relevant to trade, exchange rates, and that, in the long run, the economy is usually at full employment. In fact, when the economy is operating at full employment, as in the late 1990s, growing trade deficits affect the *distribution* of jobs rather than the overall *number* of jobs in the economy. Growing trade deficits resulted in less employment in manufacturing and more jobs in non-traded goods such as services, retail trade, and construction. . . .

The Loss of Jobs

The distribution of job losses between 1989 and 1997 closely follows changes in trade patterns. . . . The largest losses of job-supporting production in this period occurred in leather products (−66,000 job opportunities) apparel (−55,000 jobs), rubber and plastics (−38,000 jobs), furniture (−15,000 jobs), and electronic machinery (−69,000 jobs)—which included audio/video equipment (−18,500 jobs) and communications equipment (−3,700 jobs). The textile industry also experienced a major indirect effect, as it suffered a loss of output that would have supported 24,000 jobs, due to the growth of apparel imports. Note that during this period the apparel deficit was more than 10 times as large as the deficit in textiles, yet both industries suffered a similar amount of employment displacement. . . .

Between 2001 and 2003, loss of job opportunities in apparel (−24,000), textiles (−23,000), leather products (−14,000) and rubber and plastics (−15,000) fell off sharply compared to the 1989–97 period. (Note that the manufacturing trade deficit with China increased by about $45 billion in each of these periods, although the first is eight years long while the second lasted only two years.) Job displacement increased sharply in furniture (−39,000) and nonelectrical machinery (−50,000), including nearly a tripling in computers (−30,000). The largest amount of employment displacement in this period occurred in electronic machinery (−91,000 jobs), which included audio/video equipment (−28,000), communications equipment (−11,000, a near tripling), and semiconductors (−25,000).

Although the loss of job-supporting production in textiles and apparel sped up after China entered the WTO in 2001, the total remained well below levels that prevailed in the 1989–1997 base period. Since 2001 the displacement of production that could support jobs has grown most rapidly in middle- and high-technology sectors such as furniture, computers, audio/video and communications equipment, and semiconductors. China's move up the technology ladder in the opening years of the 21st century has been truly breathtaking. . . .

The displacement of domestic production in . . . advanced scientific, technological, and research industries illustrates how the demise of manufacturing brought on by growing trade deficits with China is eroding the foundations for U.S. technological leadership in many industries.

Two critical transportation equipment industries, motor vehicles and aerospace, offer a good case in point. Businesses in both of these sectors strongly supported China's entry into the WTO, claiming that the growth of the Chinese markets would increase demand for U.S. products. However, those investments have not increased U.S. employment in tandem with growing trade with China. . . . Between 1989 and 1997, the growth in the U.S. trade deficit with China had essentially no effect on the auto industry. Meanwhile the aerospace sector enjoyed substantial gains (8,100 jobs) due to its growing trade surpluses with China. However, by 2003 changing trade flows resulted in a net decline in employment-supporting production in both sectors. For motor vehicles, the NAIC[S] [North American Industry Classification System]-based data provide details on vehicle assembly, stamping, and parts trade. Overall, the industry lost production supporting 6,000 jobs between

1997 and 2001, and 5,000 jobs between 2001 and 2003, largely because of a surge in auto parts imports from China.

In aerospace, the growth in the job-creating trade surplus came to an end, and employment changes essentially ended by 2003. While the industry still maintains a substantial overall surplus in trade with China, the surplus has effectively stopped growing. It could become negative in the years ahead if parts imports begin to grow, as was the case for autos in 2003. If the United States cannot compete with China in aerospace, it is not clear which sectors could provide the foundation for closing the trade gap in the future.

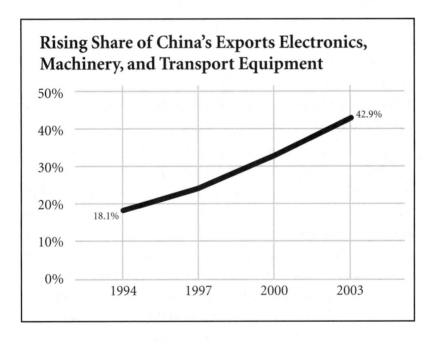

Rising Share of China's Exports Electronics, Machinery, and Transport Equipment

The Loss Affects All States

The growth of trade deficits with China displaced production supporting jobs in all 50 states and the District of Columbia throughout the study period. Exports from every state have been offset by faster-rising imports. . . .

Net employment displacement estimates between 1989 and 1997 range from a low of −334 in Alaska to a high of −81,800 in California. Other hard-hit states include Texas, New York, Pennsylvania, Illinois, North Carolina, Florida, and Ohio, each with more than 20,000 jobs lost. These states all have high concentrations of industries where a large number of plants have moved to China (textiles and apparel, furniture, computers and electrical equipment, semiconductors, and motor vehicle parts). Manufacturing industries suffered 77.8% of the trade-related jobs displacement between 2001 and 2003—364,800 good manufacturing jobs in those two years alone.

Net displacement of production-supporting employment was also negative for every state and the District of Columbia between 1997 and 2003. The magnitude of job losses in the states remained generally similar.... While job displacement in most states was modest compared to total employment, it is important to remember that the promise of new U.S. jobs was the principal justification for China's entry into the WTO....

A Continuing Challenge

Growing trade deficits with China have displaced production supporting 1.5 million U.S. jobs since 1989. The rate of job displacement is accelerating, especially since China entered into the WTO. China's entry into the world trading system was supposed to open up its vast domestic markets to products from around the world, and the United States engaged in extensive negotiations with China to ensure that it obtained its share of these benefits. These benefits have yet to materialize. Instead, multinational companies from around the world have used the protections for investment and intellectual property provided by the WTO to rapidly expand investment, production, and exports from that country. The United States remains China's primary market for exports. In just 15 years China has rapidly transformed its export profile from one dominated by clothing, shoes, and plastic products, to one in which electronics, machinery, transportation equipment, other fabricated metals, chemicals, and medical equipment account for more than half of exports. China's leading-edge industries are gaining increased market shares in the motor vehicle and aerospace sectors, which have provided the most durable foundations for the United States' industrial base for generations. That shift, in turn, reduces the demand for high-technology workers and highly skilled business professionals in the United States. It is hard to overstate the challenges posed by this export behemoth.

> *"The West may be surprised at the damage it inflicts on itself if it restricts trade with China."*

China's Trade Policies Do Not Harm the U.S. Economy

Stephen Roach

Stephen Roach is the chief economist and director of global economic analysis at Morgan Stanley, a large U.S. investment bank. An ardent detractor of critics who argue that China's booming economy is stealing jobs from U.S. industry and otherwise damaging American trade, Roach in the following viewpoint dismisses such charges as unhelpful politicking. While the sluggish U.S. economy can be attributed in part to an enormous trade deficit with China, Roach claims, cheap Chinese exports are not to blame. Roach maintains that inexpensive Chinese goods ought to be welcomed, not spurned, to keep Americans' buying power strong.

As you read, consider the following questions:

1. By what amount did U.S. imports from China exceed exports in 2004, according to the author?
2. Who does Roach believe is central to the U.S. deficit problem?

Stephen Roach, "Blaming China: Instead of Addressing Its Own Profligacy, the U.S. Risks a Ruinous Trade War," *Time International,* vol. 165, May 16, 2005. Copyright © 2005 by Time, Inc. All rights reserved. Reproduced by permission.

3. According to Roach, what factor is stabilizing China's economy?

Economics and politics often make strange bedfellows. Such is the case with America's increasingly contentious relationship with China, which has taken a sudden turn for the worse on the trade front. This poses a major risk for the global economy.

Politicians in Washington are getting nervous because of two pernicious problems facing the U.S. economy: a lackluster job market, and America's massive foreign-trade deficit. Despite a modest improvement in job creation over the past year, the U.S. remains mired in the weakest hiring cycle on record. At the same time, salaries have barely kept up with inflation—astonishing in an era of rapid productivity growth, which is normally thought to boost real wages. As a result, there is a palpable discontent in the U.S. work force that politicians do not take lightly.

To complicate matters, America's foreign-trade deficit is veering out of control. The trade gap surged to $666 billion in 2004, a record 5.7% of U.S. gross domestic product. China accounted for the largest chunk of the shortfall—U.S. imports of Chinese goods exceeded exports to China by $162 billion, accounting for about a quarter of the total trade gap.

In political circles, this is ironclad evidence of cause and effect—and China is being blamed for the tough conditions facing American workers. The Washington consensus is that Beijing's currency policy—a fixed peg of 8.3 renminbi per dollar—has given China an unfair competitive advantage that is robbing Americans of market share and jobs. Pressure is mounting for China to revalue its currency. If it doesn't do so, Congress is threatening to impose stiff tariffs on all Chinese goods sold in the U.S.[1] The drumbeat of protectionism is growing louder by the day.

1. China revalued its currency in July 2005.

Yet the economics of China bashing are not nearly as compelling as Washington believes. That's because the politicians themselves are central to this problem. America's gaping trade deficit didn't appear out of thin air. It is a direct outgrowth of an unprecedented shrinkage in overall U.S. savings, with the personal-savings rate having fallen nearly to zero and the federal government's budget having swung perilously from surplus to deficit. Lacking in domestic savings, the U.S. has had to import surplus capital from abroad in order to grow—thereby running up massive current-account and trade deficits. Were it not for a profligate Washington, America's savings rate would be higher and the trade deficit would be lower.

The politics of China bashing is misplaced for two other reasons: as long as the U.S. must trade with someone to make up for its own savings shortfall, it is to the advantage of American consumers to have access to low-cost, high-quality Chinese products. Moreover, China's export juggernaut is not what it appears to be. Fully 62% of the country's export growth over the past decade came from Chinese subsidiaries of multinationals headquartered elsewhere in the world—in Asia, Europe, and America. The West may be surprised at the damage it inflicts on itself if it restricts trade with China.

U.S. politicians have no patience for these macroeconomic arguments. In their minds, it's all about pinning the distress of beleaguered American workers on China. The recent surge of Chinese textile products into U.S. and European markets has only fueled the flames of protectionism. A mid-April procedural vote on a bill that would impose 27.5% tariffs on all Chinese goods sold in the U.S. passed the Senate by a stunning 67-33 votes, with final deliberation slated for the end of the summer. It will take deft political maneuvering to avoid a further escalation of these trade tensions between Washington and Beijing. Always in search of a scapegoat to deflect attention from its own reckless fiscal policies, Washington is not

The Economic Influence of Multinational Firms in China

American manufacturers accuse Chinese firms of stealing global market share. Yet Stephen Roach, chief economist at Morgan Stanley, points out that two-thirds of China's export growth since 1994 has come from the subsidiaries or joint ventures of foreign multinationals. China's export boom is partly due to efforts by rich-world firms to remain competitive. Had these firms not invested in China, they would have been less profitable and might have hired fewer workers at home.

Economist, *"Tilting at Dragons,"* October 23, 2003.

about to blink. Neither does China want to be put in the position of having to tamper with its stability anchor—the currency peg—especially if its financial system and economy would be put at risk.

Compromise is critical. Some adjustments in Chinese trade and currency policy, along with efforts to stimulate its anemic private consumption, would go a long way toward defusing the political tensions in Washington. Similarly, if U.S. fiscal authorities were to adopt a credible program of budgetary restraint, America's savings would improve and its excess spending would be tempered—allowing the trade deficit to begin receding.

Seventy years ago, protectionism marked one of the darkest periods in contemporary economic history: the Great Depression. Memories are dim of how destructive the endgame can be. This slippery slope must be avoided at all costs.

"After years of threatening action against Chinese piracy, it is time for the U.S. to act."

The United States Should Force China to Reduce Intellectual Property Theft

Bruce Stokes

In the following viewpoint Bruce Stokes, an international economics journalist for the National Journal, *claims that the pirating of U.S. products in China is threatening the well-being of U.S. industry. According to Stokes, everything from music CDs to industrial designs are copied and sold in China without respect or payment to their U.S. creators. Stokes maintains that since China has joined the World Trade Organization (WTO), the time is ripe to use the WTO's muscle to make the Chinese government account for its inattentiveness to piracy issues.*

As you read, consider the following questions:

1. According to Stokes, what is the piracy rate on U.S. intellectual goods in China?
2. In the author's view, why have U.S. companies been afraid to challenge the Chinese over property rights issues?

Bruce Stokes, "Time to Act on Chinese Theft," *National Journal,* vol. 37, May 14, 2005, pp. 1,491–92. Copyright © 2005 by the *National Journal.* Reproduced by permission of Copyright Clearance Center, Inc.

> 3. Instead of raising tariffs, how does Stokes suggest America tie up Chinese imports if China fails to take action on piracy?

In 1989, President George H.W. Bush placed China on an official "priority watch list," accusing Beijing of failing to protect U.S. intellectual-property rights. In late April of [2005] President George W. Bush put China on a priority watch list for its failure to crack down on intellectual piracy as it is obliged to do under the rules of the World Trade Organization [WTO], and its bilateral commitments to the United States.

As the old saying goes: "Fool me once, shame on you. Fool me twice, shame on me."

Chinese piracy of U.S. intellectual property has now been going on for more than a generation, costing American companies billions of dollars. More important, the piracy is robbing the United States of the sweetest fruits of American innovation—the profits on business software, new pharmaceuticals, and industrial designs. Such innovation is the cutting edge of this country's dwindling competitive advantage in world trade.

China Will Not Bow to Pressure

Successive U.S. administrations have promised to halt piracy. The Clinton White House went so far as to threaten the Chinese—twice—with massive economic retaliation, to no avail. Beijing's pattern is to bow to the pressure, sign new anti-piracy accords, pass new enforcement laws—and then plead implementation problems when the piracy continues.

Beijing will only take this issue as seriously as Washington does. Pat Choate, author of the recently released book *Hot Property: The Stealing of Ideas in an Age of Globalization*, which chronicles the importance of intellectual property to American prosperity since the country's founding, said in an inter-

Wilkinson. © 1995 by The Washington Post Writers Group. Reproduced by permission.

view with *National Journal*, "Innovation is our future, and we must defend the works of our innovative people."

After years of threatening action against Chinese piracy, it is time for the U.S. to act. The administration should haul China before the World Trade Organization for failing to live up to its commitments to protect intellectual property. And if the White House won't act, Congress should.

Rampant Infringement

China is a pirate's paradise. U.S. movie, CD, and software makers say that piracy rates on every form of intellectual property—copyright, patent, trademark—sold in China reaches 90 percent and higher. In other words, the makers of these intellectual properties are getting royalties on only one of every 10 of their movies, records, and programs sold in China. Chinese theft of copyrighted materials alone costs Americans at least $2.5 billion annually. This figure includes $280 million in losses by U.S. filmmakers in 2004, an increase of more than $100 million from 2003. And U.S. pharmaceutical companies say that pirating of patented drugs costs them 10 to 15 percent of their revenue in China.

"Three years into its accession to the WTO, the Chinese government still has not implemented all of its [intellectual-property] obligations," said Jesse M. Feder, director of international trade and intellectual property for the Business Software Alliance, an industry group. "Deficiencies in its law are compounded by the failure to allocate adequate resources to effectively enforce the rules that are currently in place," he said in testimony in January before the U.S.-China Economic and Security Review Commission, a congressionally created oversight body.

According to the Chinese government's own statistics, the number of cases of commercial-scale piracy forwarded for criminal investigation to its Ministry of Public Security fell from 86 in 2001 to 14 in the first half of 2004, the latest period for which figures are available. It's little wonder that the risk of criminal prosecution and prison time fails to deter Chinese pirates. Nor is it surprising that pirates see seizures of their copied DVDs and the fines imposed as simply other costs of doing business.

In their own defense, Chinese officials point out that Americans stole the designs for the automated spinning machine and the integrated textile mill from the British in the 17th and 18th centuries, creating the foundation for the U.S. textile industry, and that intellectual piracy is how all nations foster infant industries.

"Yes," acknowledged Choate, "we stole our way to industrial prominence. So we should not demagogue the Chinese. Theirs is a natural course of development. But that doesn't mean we need to be naive. Today, we need to defend our interests."

What the U.S. Needs to Do

Chinese officials are also fond of using an old saying—"The mountains are high, and the emperor is far away"—to remind complaining Americans that Beijing has only tenuous influence over what happens at the local level in many parts of China, despite American perceptions of a highly centralized Chinese state. Veteran U.S. trade negotiators reluctantly acknowledge Beijing's enforcement limitations, but argue that this is all the more reason to pressure the Chinese government to redouble its enforcement efforts.

To try to curb Chinese piracy, the U.S. Trade Representative's Office [USTR] has announced it will ask China to provide detailed documentation of its current enforcement of anti-piracy laws, including the penalties actually imposed. The office will seek new, specific commitments on protecting intellectual property and enforcing anti-piracy laws, including a significant increase in the number of criminal investigations, prosecutions, and convictions. USTR also wants to see a significant decline in the exporting of pirated goods from China to third countries. Most important, USTR has called on U.S. industry to help it develop a strong case to take China's violation of intellectual-property rights before the WTO.

The current Bush administration's passivity in the face of flagrant Chinese piracy raises doubts about its newly declared sincerity. In its first term, the Bush administration failed to file a single intellectual-property case in the WTO against anyone. With Capitol Hill growing restive about the record U.S. trade deficit with China, the timing of USTR's recent promise to get tough on China smacks of a cynical effort to ward off stronger congressional sanctions by threatening action but never really pulling the trigger.

Industry needs to call USTR's bluff.

That means that Hollywood, Microsoft, Pfizer, and others who are getting ripped off in China need to finally act. The Bush administration will not file a WTO case without their strong support, which has often been lacking because these companies have large investments in China and fear retribution. Moreover, any hint of a confrontation with Beijing will trigger cries of anguish from today's China lobby in Washington: Wal-Mart, which is dependent on imports from China, and American agribusiness, which only wants to export to China. Both will want to avoid a trade war at all costs. "Too many American corporations have such an enormous stake in the Chinese status quo," said Choate, "that none dares offend Beijing by protesting too loudly."

USTR will need all the outside support it can get to overcome traditional Washington interagency resistance to trade battles of any sort. The departments of State and Defense will reflexively oppose getting tough with China on national security grounds, and Treasury will worry about the impact of a dustup on the dollar. These are all legitimate concerns. That doesn't mean that they should prevail.

If the victims of piracy—U.S. companies—are unwilling to stand up for their own interests, USTR won't be able to make a winning case for the broader national interest in protecting American innovation.

Specific Actions

To force anyone to do anything about this problem—the administration or the Chinese—Congress needs to push the various parties.

Lawmakers must send movie, CD, and software makers the message that it's time to put up or shut up. Failure to now support a WTO case against China after years of whining should trigger serious questions on Capitol Hill about such firms' commitment to America's long-term interests. Companies need to know that such doubts have ominous implications for congressional cooperation on other issues. If Congress is unwilling to play hardball with the complainers, the administration is unlikely to be hard-nosed with the Chinese.

Washington needs to pursue a WTO suit vigorously and expeditiously. To get beyond administration foot-dragging, Congress could pass a resolution expressing its expectation that a decision to pursue a case will be made by the White

House within six months. "We should be confronting the Chinese in a meaningful way," Choate said. "We need to stress-test the WTO system to see if it works. If it doesn't work, then we need to go back to unilateral action or negotiate some other means of protecting our interests."

If no WTO case materializes, USTR can propose to China a fixed timetable for reducing across-the-board piracy rates from 90 percent or more to less than 50 percent by a certain date.

To underscore U.S. seriousness about cracking down on piracy, Congress could play the bad cop, giving USTR some leverage by passing mandatory trade sanctions against China that would go into effect if a timetable is not agreed to or not adhered to. New U.S. tariffs on imports of Chinese goods would only jack up their price, harming U.S. consumers. Congress could, instead, require a full U.S. Customs inspection of every single computer and piece of telecommunications equipment currently entering the United States from China. Current inspections are cursory and infrequent. Thorough searches would effectively tie up about $50 billion in Chinese exports, leading American importers to find suppliers in Taiwan or even back in the United States. Beijing would, of course, challenge such action at the WTO. USTR should welcome its day in court. And even if Washington lost the case, it would signal to Beijing that if China permits piracy that undermines U.S. cutting-edge industries, China will have to take some of its own medicine.

Getting tough with China about intellectual-property piracy will not be easy. A century or two ago, Britain attempted to protect its ideas and inventions from American pirates and failed. But the stakes are too high not to try.

"Intellectual-property theft threatens America's technological pre-eminence," Choate concluded in his book. "What is missing is the will of U.S. political leaders to confront those who are stealing U.S.-owned intellectual properties and, with them, the future of the American people."

> "A number of forces are nudging China into the direction of greater respect for other people's [intellectual property rights]."

China Is Taking Action Against Intellectual Property Theft

Veronica Weinstein and Dennis Fernandez

Dennis Fernandez is the head of Fernandez and Associates LLP, a law firm specializing in high-tech property rights and U.S. patent protection. In the following viewpoint Fernandez and his associate Veronica Weinstein maintain that although safeguarding intellectual property rights is still a major problem in the People's Republic of China, the Chinese government has been swift to implement laws and judicial reforms to counter piracy of both foreign and domestic products. According to the authors, the Chinese government has been prompted to take more stern measures because it has much to lose for not complying with international trade standards.

As you read, consider the following questions:

1. What does Article 57 of the Chinese Patent Law entail, according to Fernandez and Weinstein?

2. What two elements do the authors say have been recently added to the legal prosecution and punishment of patent infringers in China?

3. What was the outcome of the Nike lawsuit brought against a Chinese OEM making Nike shoes without the appropriate license, as cited by the authors?

One of the main obstacles China faced when bidding for WTO [World Trade Organization] membership was the inadequacy of its intellectual property laws. Every member of WTO is required to comply with the Agreement on Trade-Related Intellectual Property Rights (TRIPS). In its WTO accession documents, China declared its commitment to bringing its legal system in compliance with TRIPS. Since then, although the country has enacted a number of new laws and revised many existing laws and regulations to make them conform to TRIPS requirements, problems still remain.

Few would argue that strong intellectual property protection is very important for the economic future of China. One of the first decisions foreign investors have to make when considering whether or not to invest in Chinese industries is—will the potential gains of their investments overweigh the risk of losing valuable intellectual property rights (IPRs)? Despite recent efforts at reform, the general attitude amongst the companies going into China still remains thus—if you bring with you proprietary technology that can be misappropriated, expect it to be misappropriated.

Nevertheless a number of forces are nudging China into the direction of greater respect for other people's IPRs. First, the Chinese government already realizes that weak IPR protection deters foreign investments into their economy. As a result, the government has truly made a lot of progress in creating the system of intellectual property laws adequate under TRIPS. Also, emerging Chinese enterprises with home-developed products and technologies have become increasingly interested in the strengthening of domestic IPR protection. As can be expected, innovative Chinese enterprises currently suffer great losses from trademark and copyright infringement in their own country. Finally, strong Chinese IPR protection will increase the access these companies have to partnerships with overseas technology leaders.

Amendments to Existing Laws

True to its obligations under TRIPS, Beijing in recent years added, rewrote and deleted a number of IP-related laws in order to establish laws and procedures in compliance with the TRIPS Agreement.

In 1993 the Patent Law of China was amended to extend patent protection from 15 years to 20 years in accordance with TRIPS. The amendment also allowed the patenting of chemical and pharmaceutical products as well as food products, beverages, and flavorings.

The amendments made to the Chinese Patent Law in 2001 included making an unauthorized "offering for sale" a violation of patent holder's rights as required by TRIPS. It also addressed the issue of compulsory licensing, clarifying how the relative value of the license is determined for the purposes of compensation and what types of patents are subject to such licensing. Article 57 of the Chinese Patent Law now shifts the burden of proof of infringement to the defendant as required by TRIPS. . . .

China amended its Trademark Law in 2001 and amended its Implementing Rules in late 2002. . . . Protection of prior rights has been added to the Chinese Law to implement corresponding TRIPS requirements. "Well-known" marks are now protected under Articles 13 and 14 of Chinese Trademark Law. These changes are especially significant since China adheres to the "first-to-file" system and the race to the registration office can be crucial to establishing trademark rights. . . .

With the increasing popularity of the Internet, the Chinese government has also had to increase its policing of domain

Recent Changes to Chinese IPR System

Area of improvement	Current status	TRIPS compliance
Patent Term	Changed from 15 to 20 years by 1993 amendment.	Compliant
Scope of Protection	1992 amendment allowed protection of chemical and pharmaceutical products.	Compliant
Exclusive Rights	1992 and 2001 amendments added "offering for sale" and "right of import" to the list.	Compliant
Compulsory Licensing	Clarified in what situations compulsory license can be obtained.	Compensation rates can be further clarified.
Burden of Proof in Process Patent Infringement	Burden of proving non-infringement is shifted to the defendant.	Compliant
Judicial Review	Now available to review decisions of administrative board on reexamination, cancellation, and revocation of patents.	Compliant
Preliminary Injunctions	Now available.	Will see how implemented.
Statutory Damages	Up to ¥500,000 when actual damages cannot be assessed.	Might not be enough of a deterrent.
Innocent Infringer	Amendment clarified that "innocent infringer" defense is only relevant to calculation of damages.	Compliant

name violations. Although currently falling under the jurisdiction of the People's Court [the Chinese common law court], a separate dispute resolution procedure is available via the China International Economic and Trade Arbitration Centre (CIETAC).... The CIETAC arbitrates over cases where a clear confusion of domain names and registered trademarks can be shown. As of 2001, the CIETAC had issued eight rulings, five of which were in favor of the plaintiff, mostly foreign businesses such as IKEA, Proctor & Gamble, and DuPont, who were able to reclaim domain name registration rights to sites such as dupont.com.cn, ikea.com.cn, etc. . . .

Strict and Punitive Punishments

The chief complaint in the area of enforcement of IPRs in China was that even when the culprits are brought to justice, the punishment is so lax that it does not deter any future infringers or compensate the plaintiffs. Recent changes to the IP laws should somewhat alleviate this problem. Now the persons found guilty of patent, trademark or copyright infringement are required to pay actual damages or statutory damages up to ¥500,000 ($60,474) if the actual damages cannot be assessed. Actual damages can be calculated as lost profits, infringers' gains, or reasonable royalties.

Also, the Chinese customs system should be commended for their efforts to protect IPRs. Under the measures of Protection of Intellectual Property Regulations of 1995, foreign companies can register existing trademarks, copyrights and patents with the national customs system, and apply for the detention of suspected goods entering or leaving China's borders. Customs will then investigate said goods and confiscate them if they are found to be infringing, and the company may choose to pursue legal action through the courts simultaneously. Many claims of infringing goods have been thus discovered. . . .

Criminal liability was added as an available remedy to trademark infringement. Even though it is not clear to what extent criminal penalties can be brought, this is a positive development and clear indication that [the] Chinese government is serious about IPR enforcement. . . .

Software and OEMs

Additionally, all software to be sold in China now must also be registered with the Ministry of Information Industries. Under newly enacted Regulations on Computer Software Protection computer software companies can be certified as software enterprises and enjoy preferential government policies.

Finally, one of the most important decisions to come to light recently is the new literature regarding OEM manufacturers [original equipment manufacturing—vendors that sell products made by other companies but stamped with the vendor's name or logo] and trademarks issued by the Shanghai Municipal Government on May 20, 2003. In Article 6 of its Strengthening Protection of Intellectual Property Rights in Foreign Trade and Economic Cooperation Opinion, the government states that OEM manufacturers must now hold a license in order to produce items with another company's trademark. While OEM manufacturing is a blooming business in China, there are no explicit laws governing OEM and OEM-related IP issues. This Opinion disagrees with the current prevailing belief that OEM manufacturers do not need to enter into trademark agreements. In Article 3 of the same Opinion, the Shanghai Municipal Government makes it clear that even though OEM manufacturers do not "use" the trademark in China, any goods produced for the purpose of future commercial circulation falls under the "commodities" definition of the trademark laws, and must be licensed. In the case of Nike International Ltd. Vs. Cidesport & Zhejiang livestock Products Import & export Company & Jiaxing Yinxing Apparel Factory, a Chinese OEM manufacturer was producing Nike products under the authorization of a Spanish company whose Nike license only covered the country of Spain. The defendants were ordered to pay RMB300,000 and litigation expenses to Nike, whose trademark rights the court decided, were being infringed. . . .

China made tremendous changes to its intellectual property legal system. Even though the day-to-day implementation of the laws on the books often does not live up to high expectations of US businesspeople, the fact that the system of IP legislation has been put in place should be comforting. It will take time to achieve full integration of newly-adopted laws into everyday life of Chinese industry.

Periodical Bibliography

The following articles have been selected to supplement the diverse views presented in this chapter.

Keith Bradsher	"China Economy Rising at Pace to Rival U.S.," *New York Times*, June 28, 2005.
Brian Bremner et al.	"Here Come Chinese Cars: Detroit Isn't Looking in Its Rearview Mirror—Yet," *Business Week*, June 6, 2005.
Andrew Browne and Matt Pottinger	"China's Economy Grows 9.5%, Renewing Fears of Overheating," *Wall Street Journal*, January 26, 2005.
Clay Chandler	"Why China Won't Hit a Wall," *Fortune*, May 17, 2004.
Economist	"Tilting at Dragons," October 23, 2003.
Ted C. Fishman	"How to Stop a Thief—China," *USA Today*, June 15, 2005.
Jerry Flint	"Say No to China," *Forbes*, June 6, 2005.
Steve H. Hanke	"Stop the Mercantilists," *Forbes*, June 20, 2005.
Richard J. Newman	"The Rise of a New Power," *U.S. News & World Report*, June 20, 2005.
Michael Schuman	"Hey, Big Spenders! China's Expanding Consumer Class Will Provide Much-Needed Retail Therapy for a Global Economy That's Dangerously Dependent on the U.S.," *Time International* (Asia edition), May 16, 2005.
Robert Sutter	"Why Does China Matter?" *Washington Quarterly*, Winter 2004.
Laura D'Andrea Tyson	"Stop Scapegoating China—Before It's Too Late; Tariffs Won't Cure U.S. Trade Ills and May Lead to a Global Slowdown," *Business Week*, May 2, 2005.

CHAPTER 3

Is China a Military Threat?

Chapter Preface

During the Cold War, the United States considered its rival to be the Soviet Union. The Soviets had a socialist ideology that competed with Western capitalism, and they possessed a large, technologically advanced military—that included a nuclear arsenal—to support their national agenda, namely to spread communism. With the collapse of the Soviet Union, the Russian military suffered from disruption and decay, giving Americans a reason to breathe more easily. However, since the 1990s the U.S. government has turned its attention to a new potential threat. Communist China has risen to occupy the post of America's chief rival.

China's menace has much to do with its economic strength. Its powerhouse economy seems to be tarnishing the idealistic view held by many Americans that democracy and free trade alone will ensure prosperity. However, China's threat to America also has a military dimension. Fueled by its economic rise, China has been engaged in updating its mid-twentieth-century hardware—tanks, aircraft, and nuclear missiles. While critics debate how effective this modernization will be, as well as how fast it can proceed, few deny that it is taking place.

Some authorities believe that if the United States continues to upgrade its military capabilities at its current pace, China will not be able to close the technology gap for some time. As a Council on Foreign Relations Task Force noted in a 2003 report, "The balance between the United States and China, both globally and in Asia, is likely to remain decisively in America's favor beyond the next twenty years." Having the edge militarily, however, does not guarantee that the United States will not come into conflict with China's armed forces. As the task force report notes, China's military improvements have at least one short-term goal: To keep the democratic island-state of Taiwan from declaring independence. Taiwan, the haven of anti-Communist Chinese, has for decades made public its desire to be free of mainland influence, while Beijing has consistently asserted its authority over all parts of China. The United States has historically favored keeping Taiwan's democracy safe, but successive administrations since the 1950s have been careful not to spell out what measures America would take if the mainlanders ever invaded Taiwan in their bid to maintain a unified Greater China. The tension across the Taiwan Strait may, in coming years, force America's hand and ultimately put U.S. and Chinese armies at odds. Whether such a conflict will come to pass is but one of the controversies discussed in the following chapter, which analyzes the degree and status of China's military threat.

| "The [People's Liberation Army] has sought to upgrade key components of its military through purchases of foreign weapons and domestic developments."

China's Military Is Modernizing

U.S. Department of Defense

In the following viewpoint the U.S. Department of Defense maintains that China's military—known as the People's Liberation Army (PLA)—has been upgrading domestic weaponry and reorganizing its army to meet the challenges posed by more technologically advanced armies such as that of the United States. According to the report, China has beefed up its air force, air defense capabilities, and ballistic missile defenses in anticipation of short-range warfare. The Department of Defense also asserts that China has been supplementing its own domestic weapons with foreign technology, purchased primarily from the former Soviet Union.

As you read, consider the following questions:

1. According to the U.S. Department of Defense report, what aspects of its multirole aircraft is China upgrading?
2. Within how many years does the Department of Defense

U.S. Department of Defense, *Annual Report on the Military Power of the People's Republic of China,* www.defenselink.mil, May 28, 2004.

expect China to be able to field land-attack cruise missiles?

3. What are Ziyuan-1 and Ziyuan-2? What capabilities do they have, according to the author?

China's military modernization is oriented on developing the capabilities to fight and win "local wars under modern high-tech conditions." Based largely on observations of U.S. and allied operations since Operation DESERT STORM [in 1991], PLA [People's Liberation Army] modernization envisions seeking precision-strike munitions, modern command and control systems, and state-of-the-art ISR [intelligence, surveillance, and reconnaissance] platforms. Beijing sees its potential future adversaries, particularly the U.S. Armed Forces, acquiring these advanced systems, and this is a driver in PLA defensive and offensive force modernization. In addition, although the PLA views these components as significant force multipliers, it also sees them as centers of gravity that, if denied, degraded, or destroyed, could greatly hinder a modern enemy's capabilities to wage war.

In this context, the PLA has sought to upgrade key components of its military through purchases of foreign weapons and domestic development. . . .

Air Forces and Air Defenses

China continues its force-wide modernization program to improve overall combat capabilities in the next decade. Beijing continues to acquire advanced aircraft and weapons, with the goal of improving the abilities of the PLAAF [air force] and PLANAF [naval air force] to defend national airspace from attack and to interdict and strike enemy forces at greater distances from China's land and sea borders.

China continues to upgrade its air-to-air capabilities with additional Su-27/FLANKER aircraft produced from licensed Russian kits and Su-30MKK multirole fighter aircraft purchased directly from Russia. . . . China has acquired the AA-12/ADDER active-radar-guided air-to-air missile from Russia and continues to develop advanced air-to-air munitions. China flew its domestically developed FC-1 lightweight fighter for the first time during 2003. Also in development is a domestic advanced fighter, the F-10, which is to become operational in the next few years. . . . In the past 3 years [2001–2004], the pace of advanced fighter integration has quickened. Air combat tactics continue to evolve, and training is becoming more advanced, although it remains behind Western standards.

With the acquisition of multirole aircraft and advanced munitions, China is beginning to make significant strides toward improving its maritime and land-attack strike capabilities. The primary focus is on improving sensors and weapons to increase the survivability and lethality of attack airframes, allowing them to defend themselves while en route to the target and to deliver guided munitions once there. . . .

Much of China's more recent air defense modernization effort extends from Beijing's observation of Western military campaigns beginning with the Gulf War in early 1991. Employment of precision-guided munitions, stealth aircraft, and airborne C4I [Command, Control, Communications, Computers, and Intelligence] alerted Beijing to the limitations of its air defenses. Current Chinese air defense acquisitions are an effort to address these threats, as well as extend air defense coverage beyond point defense of major cities and other high-value assets. The design of the domestic HQ-9 surface-to-air missile (SAM) reportedly was influenced by these observations, as were plans to upgrade China's C4I system. Modernization is occurring in all services. . . .

Conventional Missile Systems

China has an extensive and well-established ballistic missile industrial infrastructure and has developed and produced a wide variety of land- and sea-based ballistic missiles. Beijing is concentrating on replacing liquid-propellant missiles with mobile solid-propellant ones, reflecting concerns about survivability, maintenance, and reliability. Development of land-attack cruise missiles for both theater and strategic missions is a high priority, and air-, ground-, and land-based versions of these weapons most likely will be operational within the next 5 to 10 years. Although China currently produces several types of land-, sea-, and air-launched cruise missiles, most are short range and for antiship operations. . . . In the future, China will have the option of employing conventionally armed medium-range ballistic missiles (MRBMs), which will extend the range of its conventional missile strike force. . . .

Ground Forces

The focus of Beijing's ground force modernization is to continue force reductions begun as early as the mid-1980s. Drawdowns will continue through the next decade and could reduce PLA forces by 500,000 personnel. The objective of this restructuring is to reduce the costs of supporting a large standing army, improve professionalism, and better equip and train a smaller force. The most recent and still ongoing round of force reductions began in 2003 and most likely will be complete by 2005, resulting in a drawdown of 200,000 troops. . . . During the next two decades, mechanized infantry, airborne, armored, and army aviation units will make up a much larger percentage of the force. In addition, China has recently focused on increasing the capabilities of reserve and militia units, as well as exploring ways to use civilian assets, such as ships and aircraft, to support military operations.

With the focus on PLA modernization and restructuring, the recent fielding of new equipment has been limited and, with some notable exceptions, has not appreciably improved the capabilities of China's ground forces. Even with consolidation of ground force assets into fewer units, the army remains so large as to impede rapid equipment modernization throughout its force structure. However, new equipment, although not being deployed throughout the whole of China, is being deployed to the PLA's strategically important areas, especially in the southeast.

Equipment modernization within the PLA is focused on deploying more advanced tanks, upgrading older models, and continuing extensive development of next-generation models. The PLA has several new or updated armor assets making their way into the ground force inventory, to include a light tank, an amphibious tank, and an amphibious armored personnel carrier (APC). Production of the Type 96 tank continues, with about 1,500 expected to be deployed by 2005. The Type 98, the PLA's most modern tank, is likely to remain minimally fielded in the next two decades, probably because of production costs. China also is considering upgrading older Type 69 main battle tanks with new fire-control systems [i.e., targeting and gun operation systems], engines, turrets, and explosive reactive armor and designing a next-generation infantry fighting vehicle (IFV) incorporating the upgraded version of Russian BMP-3 turret technologies (including the fire-control system). Reportedly, a prototype IFV vehicle is undergoing testing.

Beijing also has ongoing efforts in artillery development and UAV [unmanned aerial vehicles] research. The former emphasizes qualitative improvements to the PLA's artillery forces over quantitative production. Progress continues on an advanced multiple rocket launcher and a self-propelled amphibious howitzer. Interest in UAVs, mainly reconnaissance versions for use with the ground forces, underscores the PLA's requirements to increase reconnaissance and air defense capabilities. . . .

The PLA has devoted considerable resources to developing special forces, which are an integral element of China's ground force. They are expected to play an important role in achieving objectives in which limited goals, scale of force, and time would be crucial to victory in a number of military scenarios. . . .

Naval Forces

In recent years, the PLAN's [navy's] maritime mission has evolved from a static coastal defense into an "active offshore defense." This change in operations requires newer, more modern warships and submarines capable of operating at greater distances from China's coast for longer periods. To meet the challenges of its new defense strategy, China has active surface combatant, submarine, and amphibious ship construction programs, with several vessels currently under construction and plans for additional units. One of the top priorities for the PLAN during the 10th Five-Year Plan is manufacturing submarines. Where Beijing believes domestic production cannot meet defense needs it has contracted, mainly with Russia and Ukraine, to purchase weapons and equipment. . . .

To improve the PLAN's surface warfare capabilities, China has purchased two SOVREMENNYY Class destroyers from Russia, with two more on order. These provide an effective multipurpose ship capable of antiship, AAW [antiair warfare], and ASW [antisubmarine warfare] operations and are armed with 8 SS-N-22 supersonic antiship cruise missiles, 48 SA-N-7 SAMs, and 1 Ka-27 ASW helicopter. China is producing a new class of larger, more capable destroyers. Four units have been launched and are the first Chinese craft to incorporate vertically launched missile systems, possibly the domestic HQ-9 SAM. By late 2003, construction of the new-class frigate had accelerated, with production at two shipyards.

China is expanding and upgrading its submarine fleet with the purchase of four Russian KILO Class attack submarines (SSNs). The KILO is a major improvement for the PLAN over its noisy ROMEO Class submarines. In addition, the KILO may be armed with wake-homing torpedoes, which are very difficult to detect. . . .

Dangerous Trends in Future Tech Weaponry

China has long shown interest in directed energy, in particular, laser weaponry. Here, too, Beijing appears to be making progress by augmenting the existing laser blinder with a system to produce a false target to thwart laser semi-active-guided weapons. Another laser capable of blinding naval personnel may be in development.

In the space realm, the [2003 Pentagon] report notes that China is working on direct-ascent anti-satellite systems that could be fielded in 2005–10.

On the space-launch side, the Pentagon highlights China's development of a new, small solid-propellant launcher, the Kaituozhe-1.... The effort is seen as only the first of several to allow the country to launch small satellites, possibly from mobile platforms. The country's goal by 2007 is to possess the ability to put 25 tons into low-Earth orbit and 14 tons into geosynchronous orbit.

Robert Wall, Aviation Week & Space Technology,
August 4, 2003.

Space and ISR Development

Acquiring modern ISR systems remains critical to Beijing's military modernization program and supports the PLA's local wars doctrine. It also most likely is one of the primary drivers behind Beijing's space endeavors. Beijing's ongoing space-based systems with potential military applications include:

- Two new remote-sensing satellites known as Ziyuan-1 and -2, which is the Chinese name for the China-Brazil Earth Resources Satellite. Ziyuan-1B has a resolution of 19 meters and was launched in October 2003. The two

Ziyuan-2 satellites probably also are capable of collecting digital imagery and have a sun-synchronous orbit with worldwide coverage and near-real-time download of imagery of most of eastern Asia to potential ground sites in eastern and central China. Beijing also tested a new film-based imagery satellite in late 2003.

- China eventually can be expected to deploy advanced imagery, reconnaissance, and Earth resource systems with military applications. In the next decade, Beijing most likely will field radar and ocean surveillance satellites and also may deploy an improved film-based photoreconnaissance satellite. In the interim, China probably will exploit commercial SPOT, LANDSAT, RADARSAT, Ikonos, and various Russian satellite imagery systems. . . .

Acquisition of modern ISR systems remains a critical aspect of Beijing's military modernization. China is developing its ISR capabilities based on domestic components, supplemented by foreign technology acquisition and procurement of complete foreign systems. PLA procurement of new space systems, AEW [airborne early warning] aircraft, long-range UAVs, and over-the-horizon radar will enhance its ability to detect, monitor, and target naval activity in the western Pacific Ocean. It appears, from writings on PLA exercises, that this system currently lacks integration and that a fused, efficient ISR capability will not be achieved for many years.

> *"The Chinese army is still an over-sized, outdated Maoist guerrilla army with insufficient airlift, logistics, engineering, and medical capabilities to project power very far."*

The Modernizing of China's Military Is Overstated

Ivan Eland

Recent studies of China's military strength overstate the threat to the United States, argues Ivan Eland in the following viewpoint. According to Eland, U.S. Department of Defense reports charting China's advances in weaponry and its import of foreign military technology are alarmist. In Eland's view, Chinese advances cannot keep pace with American innovations. In fact, he maintains, the bulk of China's military would be obsolete on a modern battlefield. Eland is a senior fellow and director of the Center on Peace and Liberty at the Independent Institute, a public policy think tank, and editor of the institute's Independent Review.

As you read, consider the following questions:

1. According to Eland, why would the U.S. defense authorities overstate the threat of China's military modernization?

Ivan Eland, "Is Chinese Military Modernization a Threat to the United States?" *Policy Analysis,* January 23, 2003. Copyright © 2003 by the Cato Institute. All rights reserved. Reproduced by permission.

2. According to the author, how much per year do the United States and China spend on national defense?

3. In Eland's assessment, why is the Chinese navy a "sitting duck" in any conflict?

Both the Pentagon and a congressionally mandated commission recently issued studies on the Chinese military that overstated the threat to the United States posed by that force. The pessimism of both studies was understandable. The Department of Defense's study—the *Annual Report on the Military Power of the People's Republic of China* [from 2002]—was issued by a federal bureaucracy that has an inherent conflict of interest in developing assessments of foreign military threats. Because the department that is creating the threat assessments is the same one that is lobbying Congress for money for weapons, personnel, fuel, and training to combat threats, its threat projections tend to be inflated. Because China, with an economy that is seemingly growing rapidly, is the rising great power on the horizon that should shape the future posture of American conventional forces (the brushfire wars needed to combat terrorism are likely to require only limited forces), the threat from China's armed forces is critical for bringing additional money into the Pentagon. The U.S.-China Security Review Commission's work—*The National Security Implications of the Economic Relationship between the United States and China* [from July 2002]—drew at least partially on the Pentagon's effort and was written by anti-China hawks and those with a desire to restrict commerce with China. . . .

The U.S. East Asia Presence

Currently, the United States maintains about 100,000 military personnel in East Asia. That military presence is centered in Japan (41,000), South Korea (37,000), and afloat (19,000). At sea, the United States stations one carrier battle group and one Marine amphibious group forward in the region and will now ensure that a second carrier group will be there more of the time. The United States will also augment the number of nuclear submarines stationed in Guam. That military presence seems small compared to the military forces of China, which has active forces of 2.3 million.

Yet the U.S. military presence deployed forward in East Asia is only the tip of the iceberg. That presence is a symbol of U.S. interest in the region and of the world-dominant U.S. military juggernaut that could be brought to bear against the large, but largely antiquated, Chinese military during any war between the two nations.

The United States spends about $400 billion a year on national defense and alone accounts for about 40 percent of the world's defense spending. There is some dispute about how much China spends because not all of its defense spending (for example, funds for weapons research and procurement of foreign weapons) is reflected in the official Chinese defense budget. David Shambaugh, a prominent academic authority on the Chinese military, estimates total Chinese defense spending at about $38 billion per year. In the same ballpark, the International Institute of Strategic Studies' *Military Balance* estimates such spending at $47 billion per year. . . .

The $38 billion to $47 billion range is roughly what other medium powers, such as Japan, France, and the United Kingdom, spend on defense. But the militaries of those other nations are much smaller and more modern than the obsolete Chinese military, which needs to be completely transformed from a guerrilla-style Maoist people's army into a modern force that emphasizes projection of power on the sea and in the air.

The Signs of China's Weakness

The Chinese defense industry remains state owned, is grossly inefficient, and has had an abysmal track record of developing and producing technologically sophisticated weaponry. Thus, when press articles, hawkish analysts, or even the DoD [Department of Defense] notes China's pursuit of "asymmetric" technologies (ways that the weak can attack the vulnerabilities of the strong)—such as anti-satellite systems, information warfare, and radio frequency weapons (nonnuclear devices that generate electromagnetic pulses, much like those of a nuclear blast, that neutralize enemy electronics)—it does not mean that the Chinese efforts will be successful. In fact, most of the significant technological progress in the Chinese military has resulted from weapons purchased from Russia. In other words, the $1 billion or $2 billion a year China spends on Russian weapon systems—which so alarms anti-China hawks in the United States—is actually a sign of weakness in the Chinese defense industrial base. For example, China's purchase of Russian Kilo diesel submarines probably indicates that significant problems exist with China's homegrown Song-class submarine program.

Even when the Chinese buy advanced weapon systems abroad, they have difficulty integrating them into their forces. For example, the Chinese have had problems integrating the Russian-designed Su-27 fighter into their air force. As in many other militaries of the Third World, deficiencies in Chinese training, doctrine, and maintenance for sophisticated arms do not allow the full exploitation of such systems. . . .

An Outdated Military

In contrast to the thoroughly modern U.S. military, China's armed forces have been able to modernize only slowly and in pockets. According to DoD, the Chinese have a large air force—3,400 combat aircraft—but only about 100 are modern fourth-generation aircraft (for example, the Russian-designed Su-27 and Su-30). Most Chinese aircraft incorporate technology from the 1950s or 1960s. In contrast, all of the more than 3,000 aircraft in the U.S. air services are fourth-generation aircraft (F-14s, F-15s. F-16s, and F-18C/Ds), and fifth-generation aircraft (F-22s and F-18E/Fs) are already beginning production. Even Chinese pilots who fly the limited number of fourth-generation fighters get only 180 flying hours of training per year (the pilots of older aircraft get much less); U.S. fighter pilots average 205 flying hours per year.

The Chinese army is still an oversized, outdated Maoist guerrilla army with insufficient airlift, logistics, engineering, and medical capabilities to project power very far. In fact, most of the Chinese army is good only for internal security purposes. The force's equipment is antiquated—for example, most tanks incorporate technology from the 1950s. Because of nepotism, party favoritism, and poor pay compared to that in the booming private sector, the army does not get the best recruits from Chinese society, and morale of existing troops is bad. In contrast, the United States has the most potent and technologically sophisticated army in the world—with the best tank in the world (the M-1), the potent Apache anti-tank helicopter, and future plans to add the Comanche reconnaissance helicopter.

According to DoD, the Chinese navy appears to have postponed indefinitely plans to buy an aircraft carrier. In addition, DoD notes that the Chinese navy's air defense against enemy aircraft, precision-guided munitions, and cruise missiles is limited by short-range weapons (only a few of China's ships have longer-range surface-to-air missiles) and a lack of modern air surveillance systems and advanced data links to communicate that "air picture" to other ships in the fleet. The purchase of a few SOVREMENNYY-class destroyers from Russia will not alter that state of affairs significantly. In modern war, ships are vulnerable to attack from the air, and those limitations make the Chinese navy a sitting duck in any conflict. In contrast, the U.S. fleet has global dominance with 12 large aircraft carriers (Russia is the only other nation with a large aircraft carrier, which is confined to port most of the

Assessing China's Status as a Threat

There are several ways to see if China is a threat (to the United States and the international community). One is to determine if China has territorial design beyond its borders. This is certainly a disputable call. China's quest for unification with Taiwan and its claim on the South China Sea islands are cases in point. From China's perspective, these are historical losses waiting to be recovered. However, the other disputants insist that there must be room for negotiation and compromise.... A fair proposition can be made here that there is no reason to believe China would seek expansion beyond these disputes....

Realistically, any Chinese expansionist attempt will be easily offset by its geopolitical constraints. Unlike the United States, China has 15 formidable neighbors, some of whom it has unsettled border disputes with. Its approach is to mend fences and promote good neighbor relations. China has been quietly pursuing this policy for the last 20 years....

David Lai, "U.S.-China Relations: A New Start?" in The People's Liberation Army and China in Transition, *ed. Stephen J. Flanagan and Michael E. Marti.*

time), the best submarines in the world, and the most sophisticated air defense capabilities afloat (Aegis destroyers and cruisers)....

No Signs of Massive Buildup

David Shambaugh maintains that the Chinese are not engaged in a massive Soviet-style military buildup. Even the Defense Intelligence Agency and high-ranking U.S. military officials seem to agree with that assessment. According to the Defense

Intelligence Agency, by 2010, even the best 10 percent of the Chinese military will have equipment that is more than 20 years behind the capabilities of the U.S. military (equivalent to U.S. equipment in the late 1980s). The other 90 percent of the Chinese military will have even more outdated equipment. Gen. William J. Begert, the commander of U.S. Pacific Air Forces, asserted that Chinese military modernization was a "matter of concern" but not alarming. His boss, Adm. Dennis Blair, the commander of all U.S. forces in the Pacific, noted in 1999 that China would not pose a serious strategic threat to the United States for at least two decades. [China policy experts Michael O'Hanlon and Bates Gill] also conclude that the Chinese military lags behind U.S. forces by at least 20 years and that it will be that long before China's armed forces could significantly challenge the United States and allied nations in East Asia. Even DoD has admitted that "the PLA [People's Liberation Army] is still decades from possessing a comprehensive capability to engage and defeat a modern adversary beyond China's boundaries."...

Although in the last few years the Chinese have been modernizing their military more rapidly than in the past, recent hikes in the U.S. budget for national defense have been extraordinary. The increase in the U.S. budget for national defense in 2003 alone is of approximately the same magnitude as the entire Chinese defense budget (if the most probable estimates are accepted)....

China Lags Behind the United States

In conclusion, even though the Chinese military is modernizing more rapidly than in the past, the speed of the modernization is less than that of the modernization of the already vastly superior U.S. force. In other words, despite all of the clamor in the press and in the U.S. government about Chinese military modernization, the U.S. military is way ahead and the gap is actually widening (the same situation holds when U.S.

armed forces are compared with all of the other militaries in the world). When pressed, even anti-China hawks admit that Chinese military capabilities are far behind those of the United States.

> *"In the event. . .that [People's Republic of China] leaders should ever find it expedient to use tactical nuclear munitions in combat, such weapons also ensure that the [People's Liberation Army] will be able to strike crippling blows."*

China Is a Nuclear Threat

Thomas M. Kane

In the following viewpoint Thomas M. Kane argues that China poses a nuclear threat to the United States and to East Asia. Though China does not possess numerous nuclear warheads, Kane maintains that its limited stockpile is enough to devastate neighboring countries and even the western seaboard of North America. China has always considered its nuclear capabilities part of its diplomatic muscle, Kane claims, and therefore must be willing to utilize nuclear weapons to back up its foreign policy and domestic security agendas. Thomas M. Kane teaches politics and is the assistant director of the Centre for Security Studies at the University of Hull in Great Britain.

As you read, consider the following questions:

1. According to Kane, over what two major waterways does China hope to maintain an influence?

Thomas M. Kane, "Dragon or Dinosaur? Nuclear Weapons in a Modernizing China," *U.S. Army War College Quarterly*, vol. 33, Winter 2003–2004, pp. 98–113. Reproduced by permission.

2. According to a Chinese government white paper quoted in Kane's viewpoint, what nuclear weapons policy does Beijing supposedly uphold?

3. As cited by the author, how many ICBMs does the U.S. Department of Defense estimate China can build each year?

Few leaders, if any, would make the decision to deploy nuclear weapons casually. Therefore, the fact that a country possesses such arms indicates that it has important uses for them. Nevertheless, analysts of contemporary Chinese foreign policy often dismiss the nuclear arsenal of the People's Republic of China (PRC) as insignificant in size and passively defensive in purpose. Indeed, analysts of contemporary nuclear matters often fail to mention China at all. This article aims to correct these omissions by arguing that Beijing has long-term aspirations to improve its position in world politics, and that nuclear weapons play a fundamental role in its plans. . . .

Rivals to China's Influence

The PRC has ambitious foreign policy goals, many of which bring it into conflict with other powers. To begin with, the PRC, like any self-respecting state, treasures its sovereignty. Official spokesmen speak passionately about the humiliation China suffered at the hands of European powers during the 19th century, and about their country's determination never to repeat the experience. Despite the fashion for modifying the principle of national independence to accommodate international organizations and global commerce, Chinese writers define sovereignty rigidly.

Chinese leaders appreciate that their country needs to trade and cooperate with other nations, and that this will often require them to compromise. For this reason, they wish to obtain as much international influence as they can, so as to settle as many disputes as possible on their own terms. . . .

The PRC also is engaged in a large number of more specific disputes, all of which motivate it to remain militarily strong. Beijing aspires to recover Taiwan. In the South China Sea, Beijing contends with Indonesia, Thailand, Vietnam, Malaysia, the Philippines, and the Republic of China (ROC) for control over various islands. The PRC also has territorial disputes with Japan. PRC media sources sustain the idea that if Japan ever rearmed, Beijing would view it as a rival. Meanwhile, Zhao Nanqi, the director of China's Academy of Military Sciences, has commented, "We are not prepared to let the Indian Ocean become India's ocean."

Beijing also wishes to be in a position to support its Pakistani allies in their disagreements with India. The PRC government undoubtedly prizes its ability to arbitrate in Korean disputes as well. Britain's respected paper the *Daily Telegraph* reports that China has helped to secure Sudanese oilfields during Sudan's civil war, and the Chinese may wish to intervene in future African conflicts as well. By the mid 21st century, China appears likely to face severe shortages of food and energy. The PRC requires the means to secure its access to fisheries and oil reserves. In a worst-case scenario, it may need to do so by force.

The PRC's relationship with the United States is particularly strained. Chinese commentators note that the current Bush Administration has designated their country as a strategic competitor. PRC ships and aircraft have had tense encounters with American armed forces. Chinese military officers have proposed that the PRC needs to project power as far as Taiwan, the Ryukyus, the Philippines, Borneo, the Marianas, Guam, and the Carolines in order to guard its shores against overseas opponents such as America.

China's Lackluster Conventional Military Capabilities

The PRC may not wish to settle these disputes violently, but it needs to maintain the option of doing so, and China's leaders cannot feel confident that their non-nuclear forces are equal to the task. Although the various branches of the PLA [People's Liberation Army] are over two million strong, its deficiencies in troop skills, electronics, naval power, and modern aircraft make its numerical strength misleading. Not only is the PRC ill-equipped to fight the United States, it possesses only marginal advantages over such rivals as Japan, India, and the ROC....

The PRC is improving all of its forces. PRC defense budgets are difficult for outsiders to analyze, and it is difficult to tell how much of an effort Beijing is making, or how much faster it could modernize its forces if it chose to do so. One must assume, however, that the PRC is spending as much as its leaders consider desirable. From the 1980s onward, the Chinese government has been attempting to reduce the burden that defense spending imposes on its overall economy....

Despite the PLA's shortcomings, the PRC's forces are formidable, and Beijing is making substantial progress toward improving them. Beijing can and does intimidate the smaller Asian nations. Nevertheless, the PRC could not fight its major Asian rivals with any guarantee of success. In the same vein, the PRC could not refuse an ultimatum from Russia or the United States without taking an enormous gamble. These uncertainties undermine Beijing's ability both to apply and to resist pressure in international politics.

Nuclear weapons allow the PRC to take diplomatic and military positions with a much greater level of confidence. Beijing can be certain that even the United States will proceed with caution against a nuclear-armed opponent. In the event— however remote the possibility—that PRC leaders should ever find it expedient to use tactical nuclear munitions in combat, such weapons also ensure that the PLA will be able to strike crippling blows against even the strongest opponents. The PRC's nuclear arsenal also helps to prevent other powers from using or threatening to use their own nuclear weapons against China. Moreover, despite the PRC's technological and economic difficulties, Beijing is equipped to build nuclear weapons and delivery systems capable of performing all these functions at relatively little cost.

China's Nuclear Doctrine

In principle, nuclear weapons provide an excellent backstop for the PRC's national strategy. Beijing, however, denies seeing nuclear weapons in those terms. According to the PRC's national defense White Paper of 2002:

> China consistently upholds the policy of no first use of nuclear weapons and adopts an extremely restrained attitude toward the development of nuclear weapons. China has never participated in any nuclear arms race and never deployed nuclear weapons abroad. China's limited nuclear counterattack ability is entirely for deterrence against possible nuclear attacks by other countries.

When Mao Zedong initially called on his people to develop nuclear weapons, he did, indeed, seem to be thinking primarily in terms of countering the nuclear forces of others. "We also need the atom bomb," Mao stated in 1956. "If our nation does not want to be intimidated, we have to have this thing." Mao was not, however, squeamish about what nuclear weapons can do. When the Italian communist leader Palmiro Togliatti confided his fear that the Cold War might end in the nuclear destruction of Europe, Mao responded, "Who said Europe should survive?"

PRC officials continue to hint that their view of nuclear weapons is more pragmatic than documents like the White Paper might imply. . . .

Major General Yang Huan, for instance, advocates research to make nuclear weapons more useful in "actual fighting." One can interpret this remark in a variety of ways. Even a commander who is solely interested in preventing enemy attacks may want to improve his ability to fight a genuine engagement in order to improve the credibility of his deterrent threat. Nevertheless, Yang's choice of words seems significant.

Another PLA officer, Major General Wu Jianguo, has explicitly stated that his country may find nuclear weapons useful in local wars. Wu claims that Britain, America, and the Soviet Union used nuclear weapons to improve their positions in the Korean War, the Vietnam War, the Sino-Soviet dispute, the Falklands War, and the Gulf War:

> These countries threatened to use nuclear weapons in conventional wars because they believed that with nuclear weapons in hand, psychologically they would be able to hold a dominant position which would enhance troop morale and frighten the enemy on the one hand, and restrict the enemy's use of some conventional means on the other, thus changing the direction of the war.

The PRC, Wu suggests, must emulate the other nuclear powers. Throughout the 1990s, Beijing timed test firings of nuclear-capable missiles to signal its displeasure with various American foreign policy decisions and Taiwanese election results. This suggests that the PRC's leaders are willing to take Wu's advice. Wu goes on to argue that if the PRC cannot achieve its objectives through purely psychological means, it must "strive to win a victory through actual combat, so as to remove obstacles to its political, economic, and diplomatic activities. Militarily, the immense effect of nuclear weaponry is that it can serve as a deterrent force and, at the same time, as a means of actual combat." . . .

A Nuclear Arsenal

The PRC has been developing the kind of capabilities commanders such as Yang and Wu advocate. By US and Russian standards, Beijing's known nuclear arsenal appears small. Nev-

The Advent of More Sophisticated Missiles

China's nuclear arsenal will expand in number of weapons and sophistication over the next ten to twenty years. Various agencies of the U.S. government have estimated that the likely increases will range from the "tens" to "75 to 100 warheads deployed primarily against the United States." The two principal missile programs in this modernization effort will be the DF-31 and a follow-on, longer-range mobile missile, sometimes referred to as the DF-31A or DF-41. The mobile, solid-fuel DF-31 will have a range of 8,000 kilometers and carry a payload of 700 kilograms. It is expected that the DF-31 will begin deployments to replace the DF-3 [an outdated missile from the 1960s], perhaps by 2005. The development of the planned follow-on to the DF-31 the DF-31A, officially started in July 1986. This road-mobile, three-stage, solid propellant ICBM [intercontinental ballistic missile] is expected to have a range of 12,000 kilometers, capable of striking targets throughout the continental United States. If development of this missile proceeds successfully, it may begin replacing the aging DF-5 force perhaps as early as 2010.

Council on Foreign Relations, Chinese Military Power: Report of an Independent Task Force Sponsored by the Council on Foreign Relations, Maurice R. Greenberg Center for Geoeconomic Studies, *2003.*

ertheless, as the bumper sticker would have it, one atomic bomb can ruin your whole day. Although the PRC does not appear to have deployed large numbers of warheads, it has continually developed its capacity to wage nuclear war.

Even before the PRC detonated its first atomic bomb, Chinese engineers were designing intercontinental ballistic missiles (ICBMs). Beijing developed a functioning ICBM in the 1970s and deployed it in 1981. Initial versions of this missile, which was known as the DF-5, were unwieldy. . . .

During the 1980s and 1990s, the PRC improved the range, accuracy, and readiness of the DF-5. Analysts believe current models have a range of more than 13,000 kilometers, a Circular Error Probable (CEP) of 500 to 3,500 meters, and can be ready for launch in 30 to 60 minutes. In 1992, Western analysts believed the PRC had four DF-5s on alert. Three years later, the PRC had increased its arsenal to an estimated 8 to 11. As of 2003, at least 20 DF-5s are in service.

Meanwhile, the PRC has developed a solid-fueled missile known as the DF-31, which has a CEP of 300 to 500 meters. Not only can the DF-31 be ready for launch in 15 minutes, it is fully road-mobile, and analysts expect future versions to be able to travel cross-country as well. This missile's only significant handicap appears to be its 3,000- to 8,000-kilometer range, which allows it to hit America's Pacific Northwest, but nothing south or east of that. The International Institute for Strategic Studies indicates that the first DF-31 brigade became operational in 2002–03. Chinese engineers are working actively on an even more advanced design, the DF-41, which should have a longer range and a launch time of three to five minutes.

The Chinese also have developed submarine-launched ballistic missiles (SLBMs) and a nuclear-powered submarine to carry them. This submarine, the *Xia,* was out of service for the latter part of the 1990s, but may now be operational again. The PRC is working on more advanced designs for both submarines and submarine-fired missiles. Western analysts remain uncertain how quickly these projects are progressing. The PRC reportedly plans to build between four and six of the new submarines.

Although a Chinese space launch in the 1970s indicated that the PRC had developed the technology to build Multiple

Independently-targeted Reentry Vehicles (MIRVs), no Chinese missiles currently carry more than one warhead. The reason remains open for speculation. Beijing has had difficulty reducing the size of its warheads, and may find it difficult to build MIRV systems that are light enough for its missiles to carry. Alternatively, the PRC may simply prefer not to risk more than one valuable warhead on a single delivery system.

Beijing has attracted useful media attention by threatening to deploy MIRVs if the United States continues to develop its National Missile Defense (NMD) system, and the PRC's leaders may feel that they currently have more to gain by threatening to deploy MIRVs than by actually making good on the threat. The PRC has begun to develop other ways of defeating NMD as well. Chinese engineers have begun work on decoys and maneuverable warheads. Beijing also is investigating the possibility of electronically jamming NMD radar systems, and of using anti-radiation missiles to destroy such radars outright.

In addition to its ICBMs and SLBMs, Beijing has a minimum of several hundred other nuclear devices. Many may be mounted on the PRC's short- and intermediate-range ballistic missiles, which are capable of carrying either nuclear or non-nuclear warheads. The PRC built hundreds of these weapons in the late 1990s, and plans to build hundreds more in the first decade of the 21st century. As they did with their ICBMs, PRC designers have replaced liquid-fueled designs with more accurate, solid-fueled missiles capable of launching on short notice.

Both the PLA Air Force (PLAAF) and PLAN [navy] have bombers capable of dropping free-fall nuclear bombs. The US Department of Defense suggests that the PRC will soon deploy nuclear-capable cruise missiles for launch from ships and aircraft. Civilian analysts have reported that the PRC already has such missiles. The PRC also is making progress on radar-absorbent materials to make both cruise missiles and the aircraft that launch them less vulnerable to air defenses.

The PRC could use both short-range missiles and aircraft to support its non-nuclear forces in combat operations. Western observers disagree over the question of whether or not Beijing deploys purpose-built tactical nuclear weapons. More cautious analysts warn that due to Chinese secrecy and deception, it is impossible for outsiders to be certain whether the PRC has such devices. PLA units, however, have rehearsed using tactical nuclear weapons in exercises. Many analysts suggest that the PRC has nuclear artillery shells, nuclear-tipped rockets, and nuclear demolition mines. The authoritative *Jane's* publications indicate that the PRC also has nuclear mines for use at sea, nuclear torpedoes, nuclear depth charges, and nuclear anti-ship missiles.

The PRC . . . has made the command of its nuclear forces a top priority, and it has used the most advanced capabilities at its disposal to ensure that its military leaders will be able to use their nuclear forces in a timely, flexible, and controlled fashion, even under enemy attack. The PRC has situated its nuclear command posts deep underground. Key bases also benefit from a well-developed air defense system. . . .

Continued Buildup

Not only has the PRC been improving its nuclear capabilities for as long as it has had them, its military authorities have declared their intention to continue improvements. In 1993, the PLA General Staff Department (GSD) formally announced its desire to develop new generations of both tactical and strategic nuclear weapons. Although the PRC has made progress, many of the GSD's specific objectives remain to be realized, and therefore it seems safe to assume that the buildup will continue. The PRC has the infrastructure to continue developing its arsenal. US Department of Defense estimates suggest that the PRC can produce between 10 and 12 ICBMs per year, deploy as many as 1,000 new short-range missiles by the end of the decade, and triple its stockpile of nuclear warheads, all without significant new investment.

In March 2003, the Chinese politician Hu Jintao became President of the PRC. Hu already had become General Secretary of China's Communist Party in November 2002. This leadership change appears unlikely to signal any significant changes in the PRC's national strategy. Jiang Zemin, the former President, has retained control of the Central Military Commission, and Jiang's associates hold other key positions in the new government. Hu achieved his position largely by developing a reputation as a political conservative.

Reports indicate that Hu is inclined to follow his predecessors' guidance on international issues. Meanwhile, PRC media sources maintain that the global political environment remains largely the same as it has been for decades. To writers in *Beijing Review,* even the Bush Administration's National Security Strategy of preventive attack is "just old wine in a new bottle." The PRC's nuclear policy has remained consistent for close to 40 years. If PRC leaders do not feel that their external environment has changed, they have few reasons to change that policy.

> "In the midst of a crisis, any attempt by Beijing to ready its ballistic missiles for a first strike against the United States, let alone to actually fire one, would be suicide."

China Is Not a Nuclear Threat

Jeffrey Lewis

Jeffrey Lewis is a research fellow at the University of Maryland's Center for International and Security Studies. In the following viewpoint Lewis maintains that China's nuclear arsenal is very small in comparison to that of the United States and other developed nations. Lewis argues that most Chinese nuclear missiles still lack the range to be a significant threat to the United States or other nations outside Southeast Asia should a confrontation occur. For these reasons, Lewis claims, it is disturbing that the U.S. government would try to make more of the potential danger than is prudent.

As you read, consider the following questions:

1. How does Lewis refute the claim that China's new submarine-launched Julang-2 ballistic missile can carry three to eight separate warheads?

2. According to Lewis, what international legislation stops

Jeffrey Lewis, "The Ambiguous Arsenal," *Bulletin of the Atomic Scientists,* vol. 61, May/June 2005, pp. 52–59. Copyright © 2005 by the *Bulletin of the Atomic Scientists,* Chicago, IL 60637. Reproduced by permission.

China from testing new nuclear warheads?

3. Why did Secretary of Defense Donald Rumsfeld criticize calls to reduce America's nuclear arsenal below 1,700 missiles, in the author's opinion?

If you read the *Washington Times*, in addition to believing the Iraqi weapons of mass destruction are hidden somewhere in Syria, you might believe that [according to a January 4, 2002, article] "China's aggressive strategic nuclear-modernization program" was proceeding apace. If munching on freedom fries at a Heritage Foundation luncheon is your thing, you might worry [as stated in a June 26, 1998, Heritage Foundation *Backgrounder* article] that "even marginal improvements to [China's intercontinental ballistic missiles (ICBMs)] derived from U.S. technical know-how" threaten the United States.

So, it may come as a shock to learn that China's nuclear arsenal is about the same size it was a decade ago, and that the missile that prompted the *Washington Times* article has been under development since the mid-1980s. Perhaps your anxiety about "marginal improvements" to China's missile force would recede as you learned that China's 18 ICBMs, sitting unfueled in their silos, their nuclear warheads in storage, are essentially the same as they were the day China began deploying them in 1981. In fact, contrary to reports you might have ... read that Chinese nukes number in the hundreds—if not the thousands—the true size of the country's operationally deployed arsenal is probably about 80 nuclear weapons.

The Rationale for Exaggerating China's Nuclear Capability

Estimating the size, configuration, and capability of China's nuclear weapons inventory is not just an exercise in abstract accounting. The specter of a robust Chinese arsenal has been cited by the Bush administration as a rationale for not making deeper cuts in U.S. nuclear deployments. Likewise, opponents of the Comprehensive Test Ban Treaty (CTBT) point to China in making the case for maintaining U.S. deterrent capabilities. Others portray China's modernization program as evidence of the country's increasingly hostile posture toward Taiwan— adding a sense of urgency to developing missile defenses. And, more recently, these concerns have raised the temperature in transatlantic relations as the European Union contemplates lifting the arms embargo imposed on China in the wake of the Tiananmen Square massacre [in 1989].

The true scope of China's nuclear capabilities are hidden in plain sight, among the myriad declassified assessments produced by the U.S. intelligence community. Yet, such analyses have run afoul of conservative legislators, who express dismay when threat assessments don't conform to their perceptions of reality. Congressional Republicans, for instance, in 2000 created the China Futures Panel, chaired by former Gen. John Tilelli, to examine charges of bias in the CIA assessments of China. In 2002, Bob Schaffer, a Republican congressman from Colorado, complained about the latest National Intelligence Estimate (NIE) of foreign ballistic missile development in a letter to CIA director George Tenet: "The lack of attention to the pronounced and growing danger caused by China's ballistic missile buildup, and its aggressive strategy for using its ballistic missiles cannot go unchallenged. The report is misleading, and, because it understates the magnitude of threat, is profoundly dangerous."

Consequently, many defense analysts simply ignore what the intelligence community has to say. For example, two scholars in a peer-reviewed international security journal cited *Jane's Strategic Weapon Systems* to suggest that China's future submarine-launched ballistic missile (SLBM)—the Giant Wave, or Julang-2 (JL-2)—may carry "three to eight multiple independent reentry vehicles." They failed to mention the consensus judgment of the U.S. intelligence community that Chinese warheads are so large that it is impossible to place more than one on the JL-2.

In another instance, a student from the National University of Singapore posted an essay on a web site claiming that China had more than 2,000 warheads. His figure was based on amateurish fissile material production estimates that incorrectly identified several Chinese fissile material facilities. (Classified estimates by the Energy Department, leaked to the press, estimate the Chinese plutonium stockpile at 1.7–2.8 tons. Assuming 3–4 kilograms of plutonium per warhead, China could deploy, at most, a nuclear force of 400–900 weapons.) Despite such obvious mistakes, experts from the Heritage Foundation, the Institute for Defense Analyses, the Institute for Foreign Policy Analysis, and the Centre for Defence and International Security Studies all cited the Singapore essay to suggest that China might have substantially more nuclear warheads than widely believed. David Tanks, then with the Institute for Foreign Policy Analysis, called the essay "convincingly argued."

Iraq debacle or not, the estimates of the U.S. intelligence community are still a better place to start than, say, some college kid's essay posted on the internet. These analysts have unparalleled access to the full array of information-gathering technology available to the federal government. For example, the intelligence community monitors ballistic missile tests with satellite images to detect test preparations, signals intelligence sensors to intercept telemetry data, and radars to track missile launches and collect signature data on warheads and decoys. No comparable unclassified source of such data exists, unless it is released by the government conducting the tests. . . .

The Minimum Means of Reprisal

Beijing doesn't publish detailed information about the size and composition of its nuclear forces. With a very small nuclear arsenal relative to the United States and Russia, China seems intent on letting ambiguity enhance the deterrent effect of its nuclear forces. Chinese force deployments suggest that Beijing's leadership believes that even a very small, unsophisticated force will deter nuclear attacks by larger, more sophisticated nuclear forces. While some Western analysts spent the Cold War fretting about the "delicate balance of terror," the Chinese leadership appears to have concluded that technical details such as the size, configuration, and readiness of nuclear forces are largely irrelevant. China's declaration that it would "not be the first to use nuclear weapons at any time or under any circumstances" reflects the idea that nuclear weapons are not much good, except to deter other nuclear weapons. In deciding what sort of nuclear arsenal to build, China settled on what Marshal Nie Rongzhen, the first head of China's nuclear weapons program, called "the minimum means of reprisal."

China's reluctance to provide numerical information about its nuclear forces relaxed a bit [in the spring of 2005], when its foreign ministry released an April 2004 statement that, "Among the nuclear weapon states, China . . . possesses the smallest nuclear arsenal." That statement suggests China possesses fewer than 200 nuclear weapons, the generally accepted size of the British nuclear arsenal. . . .

Estimates provided by many [Western] nongovernmental organizations—such as the Council on Foreign Relations, the Natural Resources Defense Council, and the International Institute for Strategic Studies (IISS)—are . . . higher (albeit, not as high as their more zealous conservative counterparts). They typically describe the People's Republic of China as the world's third largest nuclear power, ahead of Britain and France, with 400 or so warheads. Such estimates often assume deployment of three other categories of nuclear weapons—aircraft-delivered weapons, SLBMs, and tactical nuclear weapons.

Yet, in the 1980s, the Defense Intelligence Agency (DIA) found no evidence that China had deployed nuclear bombs to

China's Commitment to a No-First-Use Policy

China has consistently advocated the complete prohibition and thorough destruction of nuclear weapons. On the very first day it came into possession of nuclear weapons, China solemnly declared that at no time and under no circumstances would it be the first to use such weapons. Later, China undertook unconditionally not to use or threaten to use nuclear weapons against non-nuclear-weapon states or nuclear-weapon-free zones, and has consistently urged all nuclear-weapon states to enshrine these commitments in a legal form. China has always exercised utmost restraint on the development of nuclear weapons, and its nuclear arsenal is kept at the lowest level necessary for self-defense only. China holds that countries having the largest nuclear arsenal bear a special and primary responsibility toward nuclear disarmament, and that they should take the lead in drastically reducing their nuclear arsenals and destroy the reduced nuclear weapons. China welcomes the new treaty signed by the US and Russia on the reduction of their offensive strategic weapons, and hopes that these two countries will adopt effective measures to ensure the "verifiability" and "irreversibility" of nuclear disarmament, and continue to further the process of nuclear disarmament, so as to genuinely promote world peace and stability.

China's National Defense in 2002, *Government of the People's Republic of China white paper, December 9, 2002.*

airfields and, based on the antiquity of the aircraft, concluded that China did not assign nuclear missions to any of its planes—a conclusion reiterated in a declassified 1993 National Security Council report. The most recent edition of the

Pentagon's *Chinese Military Power* suggests that China has yet to deploy the Julang-1 (JL-1) ballistic missile on its solitary ballistic missile submarine. And, in 1984, the DIA acknowledged that it had "no evidence confirming production or deployment" of tactical nuclear weapons. To the contrary, *Chinese Military Power* notes that the country's short-range ballistic missiles are conventionally armed, thereby freeing Beijing from "the political and practical constraints associated with the use of nuclear-armed missiles."

Room for Expansion?

Over the next 15 years, the intelligence community expects China's ICBM force to expand from 18 to 75–100 strategic nuclear warheads targeted primarily against the United States and from 12 shorter-range ballistic missiles capable of reaching parts of the United States to "two dozen."

Beijing's modernization plan centers on a mobile, solid-fueled ballistic missile under development since the mid-1980s called the Dong Feng (DF) 31. The intelligence community believes the DF-31 could be deployed during the next few years. Since 2002, IISS has cited "reports" that the DF-31 is deployed, but that assessment appears based on a pair of 2001 news stories in the *Taipei Times* and *Washington Times,* neither of which actually claims the missile is deployed.

The intelligence community believes China is also developing follow-on versions of the DF-31: the extended-range DF-31A to replace the DF-5 (currently its longest-range ICBM) and a submarine-launched version (JL-2). The DF-31A may have a range of 12,000 kilometers and could be deployed before 2010. China is also designing a new nuclear ballistic missile submarine to carry the JL-2, which is expected to have a range of more than 8,000 kilometers. China will likely develop and test the JL-2 and the new sub (Type 094) later this decade.

One senior intelligence official described the 75–100 warhead estimate to the *New York Times* [in a May 28, 2000, article]: "[China would] add new warheads to their old 18 [DF-5s], transforming them from single-warhead missiles to four-warhead missiles," or "double the size of their projected land-based mobile missiles." The estimate of 75 warheads assumes that China will supplement its existing ballistic missile force with the DF-31 ICBMs; the estimate of 100 warheads is based on the assumption that China would build half as many DF-31 ballistic missiles, but place multiple warheads on existing DF-5 ICBMs.

China has not placed multiple warheads on its silo-based ICBMs and has not begun to deploy the DF-31. Therefore, these predictions are little more than informed speculation, based on how the intelligence community imagines China *might* respond to missile defense and other changes in U.S. nuclear posture. Past intelligence community estimates, however, have overstated future Chinese ICBM deployments. The number of Chinese strategic ballistic missiles has actually declined, from 145 in 1984 to 80 today.

China tested its smallest nuclear warhead from 1992–1996. Developed for China's DF-31 ICBM, NASIC [National Air and Space Intelligence Center] estimated that the reentry vehicle has a mass of 470 kilograms—too heavy to place more than one on any of China's solid-fueled ballistic missiles. Placing multiple warheads on China's solid-fueled ballistic missiles would probably require Beijing to design and test a new warhead, which is currently prohibited by China's signature on the CTBT.

Dangerous Incentives

So, let's review: China deploys just 30 ICBMs, kept unfueled and without warheads, and another 50–100 MRBMs [medium-range ballistic missiles], sitting unarmed in their garrisons. Conventional wisdom suggests this posture is vulnerable and invites preemptive attack during a crisis. This minimal arsenal is clearly a matter of choice: China stopped fissile material production in 1990 and has long had the capacity to produce a much larger number of ballistic missiles. The simplest explanation for this choice is that the Chinese leadership worries less about its vulnerability to a disarming first strike than the costs of an arms race or what some Second Artillery officer might do with a fully armed nuclear weapon. In a strange way, Beijing placed more faith in Washington and Moscow than in its own military officers.

Washington has never reciprocated that trust. Instead, the United States has embarked on a major transformation of its strategic forces that is, in part, driven by concern about the modernization of China's strategic forces. President Bill Clinton reportedly directed U.S. Strategic Command in 1998 to include plans for strikes against China in the U.S. nuclear weapons targeting plan. The 2001 Nuclear Posture Review (NPR) identified China as one of seven countries "that could be involved in an immediate or potential contingency" with nuclear weapons.

Chinese strategic forces are increasingly supplanting Russia as the primary benchmark for determining the size and capabilities of U.S. strategic forces—at least in administration rhetoric. China's nuclear arsenal is reflected in the 2001 NPR in two ways. First, the review recommends reducing the 6,000 deployed U.S. nuclear weapons to no less than 1,700–2,200. In response to criticism that these cuts didn't go low enough, Defense Secretary Donald Rumsfeld warned that further reductions might encourage China to attempt what he termed a "sprint to parity"—a rapid increase in nuclear forces to reach numerical parity with the United States.

Second, the 2001 NPR recommends the addition of ballistic missile defenses and non-nuclear strike capabilities to help improve the ability of the United States to extend nuclear deterrence to its allies. Here too, concern over China's arsenal lurked in the background. Shortly before he was nominated as Deputy Assistant Secretary of Defense for Forces Policy (with responsibility for overseeing the NPR), Keith Payne argued that the United States, in a crisis with China over Taiwan, must possess the capability to disarm China with a first strike if U.S. deterrence is to be credible....

Yet, if the United States were truly interested in discouraging a Chinese sprint to parity or the development of a Chinese ballistic missile force that could undertake coercive operations, the president would disavow the vision for nuclear forces outlined in the NPR. The Chinese leadership chose their arsenal in part on the belief that the United States would not be foolish enough to use nuclear weapons against China in a conflict. By asserting that Washington *may be* that foolish, and by attempting to exploit the weaknesses inherent in China's decision to rely on a small vulnerable force, the NPR creates incentives for Beijing to increase the size, readiness, and usability of its nuclear forces.

Larger, more ready Chinese nuclear forces would not be in the best interests of the United States. In the midst of a crisis, any attempt by Beijing to ready its ballistic missiles for a first strike against the United States, let alone to actually fire one, would be suicide. The only risk that China's current nuclear arsenal poses to the United States is an unauthorized nuclear launch—something the intelligence community has concluded "is highly unlikely" under China's current operational practices. That might change, however, if China were to adopt the "hair trigger" nuclear postures that the United States and Russia maintain even today to demonstrate the "credibility" of their nuclear deterrents. China might also increase its strategic forces or deploy theater nuclear forces that could be used early in a conflict—developments that might alarm India, with predictable secondary effects on Pakistan.

So far, none of this has happened. Chinese nuclear forces today look remarkably like they have for decades. The picture of the Chinese nuclear arsenal that emerges from U.S. intelligence assessments suggests a country that—at least in the nuclear field—is deploying a smaller, less ready arsenal than is within its capabilities. That reflects a choice to rely on a minimum deterrent that sacrifices offensive capability in exchange for maximizing political control and minimizing economic cost—a decision that seems eminently sensible. The great mystery is not that Beijing chose such an arsenal, but that the Bush administration would be eager to change it.

| "Of all the threats to security and US interests in Asia, the confrontation across the Taiwan Strait is surely the most perilous over the long run and has the greatest potential for erupting into a war between the United Sates and China."

War with China over Taiwan Is Possible

Richard Halloran

In the following viewpoint Richard Halloran, formerly an Asia correspondent for the New York Times *and currently a freelance journalist who writes about Asian security and U.S. policy toward Asia, argues that war with China over Taiwan is possible. Taiwan's desire to assert its independence coupled with China's policy to thwart such a move make an eventual clash conceivable, he maintains. Because the Taiwan Relations Act of 1979 requires the United States to take seriously a military threat to Taiwan, Halloran contends that a conflict over the island's future would most likely bring America into the fray.*

As you read, consider the following questions:

1. According to Halloran, in what way did Taiwan become an "Asian tiger" after the death of its Nationalist leader Chiang Kai-shek?

Richard Halloran, "Taiwan," *Parameters*, vol. 33, Spring 2003, pp. 22–34. Copyright © 2003 by Richard Halloran. Reproduced by permission.

2. Who is Chen Shui-bian, and, according to the author, what is his proposed "Asian democratic alliance"?

3. In Halloran's view, why is Taiwan's defense tied to America's credibility in Asia?

Of all the threats to security and US interests in Asia, the confrontation across the Taiwan Strait is surely the most perilous over the long run and has the greatest potential for erupting into a war between the United States and China. As Kurt Campbell and Derek Mitchell of the Center for Strategic and International Studies in Washington wrote [in *Foreign Affairs*] in the summer of 2001, "Perhaps nowhere else on the globe is the situation so seemingly intractable and the prospect of a major war involving the United States so real."

Today, that outlook is even more dire as China, Taiwan, and the United States have hardened their positions, even if the rhetoric has been less harsh for the most part recently. China has new leaders who cannot afford to be less than adamant on the Taiwan question. Taiwanese leaders have been pushing their island further away from the mainland, drawing Chinese warnings that military force would be employed if Taiwan goes too far. The United States, under President [George W.] Bush, has demanded that any settlement of the Taiwan question be peaceful and in accord with the wishes of the people of Taiwan. Beyond that, the Administration has repeatedly reminded the Chinese of US obligations under the Taiwan Relations Act of 1979 to help Taiwan defend itself.

All of this has reduced diplomatic maneuvering room and made for a situation in which a miscalculation could cause an eruption. Admiral Thomas B. Fargo, then Commander of US Pacific Command, told a gathering last summer [2003] at the East-West Center, a research organization in Hawaii, that among the issues concerning him was "a miscalculation between strategic rivals, and I'm talking about China and Taiwan and India and Pakistan here." Earlier, the Admiral told Congress that among the "fundamental challenges" he would confront was "the potential for accelerated military competition or, worse, gross miscalculation between India and Pakistan, China and Taiwan, or some other strategic rivals." His predecessors, Admirals Dennis Blair and Joseph Prueher, are known to have been concerned about the same possibilities. . . .

Bush and Jiang Acknowledge the Problem

Moreover, the dispute over Taiwan is dynamic and volatile, the focal point of maneuvering between Taipei, Beijing, and Washington. It is in constant danger of igniting, as evidenced by the strains after the US accidental bombing of the Chinese Embassy in Belgrade in May 1999 and the collision of a Chinese fighter with a US Navy EP-3 over the South China Sea in April 2001. Each incident brought tensions to a boil. The year 2002, culminating in the summit meeting between President Bush and President Jiang Zemin of the People's Republic of China (PRC) was relatively quiet, the Chinese perhaps having concluded that the United States is not the paper tiger that the revolutionary leader Mao Zedong once thought.

The underlying conflict has not gone away, however. Subtle evidence surfaced in the press briefing after President Bush and Jiang met at the Bush ranch in Crawford, Texas, in October 2002. Despite the smiles and polite rhetoric, President Bush noted, "It is inevitable that nations the size of the United States and China will have differences." President Jiang agreed: "It is only natural for China and the United States to disagree from time to time."

During their summit, President Bush broached the subject of Taiwan after discussing China's spotty record on human rights, suppressing minorities, and silencing dissent. He told Jiang that his China policy was based on the Taiwan Relations Act and the Three Communiqués of 1972, 1979, and 1982 between the United States and China, all of which call for a peaceful settlement of the dispute. "We intend to make sure that the issue is resolved peacefully," he said.

President Jiang meanwhile put Taiwan high on his list of priorities, saying, "We have had a frank exchange of views on the Taiwan question, which is of concern to the Chinese side." He asserted, "China has never engaged in expansion nor sought hegemony," which even the most cursory reading of Chinese history will show is not so. . . .

China's Outlook

[A] potential Sino-US confrontation arises from Beijing's obsession with the island off its southeastern coast that was long a backwater of the Chinese empire with a distinctive language and culture. Taiwan was ceded to Japan in the Treaty of Shimonoseki after Japan defeated China in the Sino-Japanese War of 1894–95 and was part of the Japanese Empire until 1945, when World War II ended with the surrender of Japan. Japan relinquished sovereignty over Taiwan in the San Francisco Peace Treaty of 1951 but never said to whom sovereignty passed.

Meantime, the Nationalist Chinese forces of Generalissimo Chiang Kai-shek were run off the mainland by Mao Zedong's Communists and took refuge on Taiwan in 1949. Chiang's regime claimed to be the sole and legitimate government of all China and vowed to retake the mainland. After his death in 1975, that dream faded. Successive governments in Taipei gradually turned to democracy and economic development, making Taiwan an "Asian tiger" along with South Korea, Hong Kong, and Singapore.

The communist government in Beijing wants possession of Taiwan for several reasons:

- *Surging nationalism.* National pride is perhaps the prime motive for capturing Taiwan. Chinese leaders see Taiwan as the last vestige of the humiliation by Japan and the West during the colonial period when imperial powers carved China into spheres of influence. China reclaimed Hong Kong, the British colony, in 1997, and Macau, the Portuguese colony, in 1999. Taking Taiwan would complete that trilogy and end the civil war with the Nationalists.

- *Political embarrassment.* Taiwan has become a democracy, even if a fragile one, over the last decade. Despite the internal controls exerted by the Beijing regime, it cannot shield the Chinese people from the example of democratic progress in Taiwan, which the Communist Party fears could jeopardize its grip on power. David Zweig of the Hong Kong University of Science and Technology has written that the Chinese people are not so politically apathetic as some argue.

- *Subversive freedom.* Political observers in Taipei have noted that visitors from China have been impressed with the freedom of the Taiwanese experience. "They are surprised by the freedom we have to work where we want, to change jobs, to live where we want, to read different views in the newspapers, and things like that," said a Taiwanese scholar. Beijing is unhappy when those visitors return to China with what the authorities consider to be subversive views.

- *Spreading separatism.* An editor of a trade journal sat in a coffee shop in Shanghai several years ago and explained her personal dilemma over Taiwan. "I think Taiwan should be part of China," she said, "but I don't think it's worth fighting over. On the other hand, if we give up Taiwan, the Tibetans will push harder to separate from China and so will the Uighurs in Xinjiang [another province pushing for independence]." She lamented, "What will become of my country?"

- *Strategic geography.* Chinese leaders see Taiwan as a critical link in a chain of containment that begins with

US forces in Korea and Japan and runs south through Taiwan to the Philippines, Thailand, and Australia, nations with which the United States has security treaties. The United States is committed through the Taiwan Relations Act to provide Taiwan with sufficient arms to defend itself. Beijing seeks to break that chain and to project power into the Pacific. Moreover, Taiwan sits astride the two northern channels into the South China Sea, most of which China claims as internal waters.

- *Economic capacity.* Absorbing Taiwan's vibrant economy and technological prowess, especially in electronics, would be a plus for the troubled Chinese economy. China has already benefited from Taiwanese investment and trade. The government in Taiwan, however, has sought to discourage investment on the mainland so that Taiwan does not become too closely integrated with China economically; it seeks to steer investment toward Southeast Asia.

- *Diverting attention.* Some China hands believe that Chinese leaders play up the Taiwan issue to divert attention from China's political struggles and economic difficulties. China is passing through a tense transition from the Third Generation to the Fourth Generation of leaders at the same time corruption is rampant, the banking system is riddled with bad loans, industrial productivity lags (especially in state-owned enterprises), and 125 million people—equal to the population of Japan—are in motion every day looking for work.

In sum, China's leaders see bringing Taiwan into the PRC as a crucial step in establishing Chinese influence over East Asia and in driving the United States from the Western Pacific. That explains the relentless drumbeat emanating from Beijing. Taiwan is the central question in every meeting between Chinese and American officials, in every academic gathering that includes Chinese scholars, and in many private conversations with Chinese visitors to the United States.

Backing Up Its Threats

The Chinese pound the issue to the point of tedium. Hu Jintao, who has succeeded Jiang as Chairman of the Communist Party, told Deputy Secretary of State Richard Armitage in August [2002]: "The separatist activities of 'Taiwan independence forces' pose the gravest threat to peace and stability across the Taiwan Strait, and [are] an element of sabotage to peace and stability in the Asian-Pacific region." Quoted in the *People's Daily*, Hu said: "We will never allow the independence of Taiwan nor tolerate the harm caused by separatist forces in Taiwan to China's sovereignty and territorial integrity."

Bonnie S. Glaser, a respected China watcher, has written that mainland officials harbor "no illusions" about Taiwan and have called for increased pressure on Washington to rein in Taiwan's pro-independence leanings. China has accelerated the development of credible military options intended to deter formal separatism and to prepare for the use of force should China's leaders deem that necessary.

Therein lies the danger of miscalculation. Chinese political leaders and senior officers of the People's Liberation Army have said repeatedly that China will attack Taiwan if the government in Taipei declares independence. That has been coupled with Chinese contentions that the United States will not fight for Taiwan because few Americans see Taiwan as important. More than one Chinese has asked, "Why should Americans care about what happens to Taiwan?"

American military leaders have cautioned the Chinese that they would be mistaken in thinking the United States will back down if confronted by a Chinese military threat to Taiwan. Leaders of the Pacific Command have told the Chinese directly that their command stands ready "to respond to any potential crisis, including the use of force against Taiwan by China." . . .

Taiwan's Sense of Sovereignty

In Taiwan itself, people have become increasingly intent on remaining detached from the mainland, even if they are not ready to declare independence for fear of provoking the PRC. There is a growing sense of Taiwanese identity and a desire for self-determination. Democracy has taken hold, even if its roots are still in shallow ground, and that has reinforced the Taiwanese quest to retain charge of their own future. . . .

Nearly 88 percent of those polled in a Taiwan Social Change Survey in 2000 responded that they considered themselves Taiwanese or Taiwanese-and-Chinese, up from 75 percent only five years before. Just eight percent saw themselves as only Chinese, down from 19 percent in 1995. . . .

A critical figure is Chen Shui-bian, the intense, shrewd, and energetic 52-year-old President of the Republic of China on Taiwan. Since taking office, Chen has sought to expand what the Taiwanese call their "international space," which means keeping their distance from the PRC while seeking greater recognition abroad. Chen, combining domestic politics, diplomacy, economic policy, and military acquisition, has put Beijing on the defensive again and again by proposing talks intended to lower tensions. Beijing, however, has said it would talk only if Chen accepted their version of the "One China" principle, which means acknowledging Chinese sovereignty over Taiwan. Chen has countered by offering talks with no conditions set. A standoff has been the result. . . .

Chen has proposed that democratic nations in Asia form an "Asian democratic alliance" to help persuade authoritarian nations such as China to become democratic. "For Taiwan, as a prime example of the global third wave of democratization, we are willing to cooperate with like-minded countries to contribute to the consolidation of Asian democracy and to promote democracy throughout the continent, notably in China," he told the Asia-Pacific Democratic Cooperation Forum in Taipei.

Similarly, Chen has sought to strengthen Taiwan's ties to several nations by proposing free trade agreements with the United States, Japan, Singapore, Panama, and New Zealand. Taiwan joined the World Trade Organization at the same time as the PRC in 2002. . . .

In short, President Chen has led a concerted effort to gain international recognition and to move closer to formal independence. Therein lies the danger of miscalculation. If Chen misjudges where the brink might be and either treads too close or steps over the line, that would almost certainly provoke a vigorous Chinese response, including the use of military force.

Where the United States Stands

This is the situation in which the United States finds itself, largely by President Bush's choice. By any measure, he has shown the strongest support for Taiwan of any American President since Richard Nixon traveled to Beijing 30 years ago. . . .

Bush's pledge that the United States would do "whatever it takes" to help Taiwan defend itself is well known. So is his Administration's permit for Taiwan to buy modern weapons for $4 billion. . . .

Less well known has been a thorough revision of US war plans to help Taiwan repel an unprovoked attack by the PRC. Under Admiral Blair, who retired as Commander of the Pacific Command in May 2002, those plans were updated to account for the Chinese acquisition of modern Russian warplanes and warships and addressed weaknesses in Taiwan's defenses.

At the same time, Blair told Chinese leaders that US forces were prepared to fight on behalf of Taiwan if a political decision was made to do so and that the defense of Taiwan would be worth risking American lives. Whether Chinese leaders believed him is open to question, as they have asserted that the United States would not take that risk.

Admiral Blair's relief, Admiral Fargo, who took command in May 2002, indicated Taiwan's defensive flaws in response to questions from Congress. He ticked off a list that included command, control, communications, computers, intelligence, surveillance, and reconnaissance. Fargo said the United States should help in "improving their integrated sea and air defense capability and assisting them in the integration of their components into an effective joint defense." . . .

The Ebbing of Strategic Ambiguity

The expansion of American military ties with Taiwan has been acccompanied by a fading of the "strategic ambiguity" that previously marked American policy. That ambiguity was intended to keep Beijing and Taipei guessing about how the United States would respond to hostilities across the Taiwan Strait. Beijing was not to know if the Americans would charge across the sea, nor was Taiwan to have any assurance that the cavalry would ride to the rescue. The intent was to deter both sides from rash action.

As strategic ambiguity has ebbed, positions have hardened all around. Bush officials have emphasized the Taiwan Relations Act, or TRA, which says that an assault on Taiwan would be "of grave concern to the United States." The TRA was passed by Congress over President Carter's objections after he switched diplomatic ties to Beijing from Taiwan, and President Bush has been more forceful than his predecessors in emphasizing the TRA. It is the law of the land and takes precedence over the Three Communiqués, a point the Chinese chose not to acknowledge. . . .

The Risk of Misinterpreting China's Ambiguous Stance

China says that it wants stability across the Taiwan Strait, that it can postpone final resolution of the cross-strait issue for a long time, that it is developing its regional military capabilities solely to deter Taiwanese independence, and that it will use force if necessary to prevent or reverse a declaration of independence. But these positions have not served China's interests well, because it has failed to make clear exactly what "declaring independence" involves.

By not doing so, Beijing has risked miscalculation by a Taiwanese leadership that does not want to provoke a military response but continues to push the envelope just short of one. The fact that for more than a decade Taiwan's leaders have declared Taiwan to be "an independent, sovereign country" without dramatic consequences adds to the confusion. Beijing's stance now runs the risk that Taiwanese President Chen Shui-bian will consider China's threats a bluff. (Chen's pro-independence predecessor Lee Teng-hui, for example, has said that Beijing is nothing more than a "paper tiger.") Ironically, Beijing's position also enhances the stature and leverage of the pro-independence elements in Taiwan. Since China says war and peace will be determined by what these individuals say and do, they attract enormous domestic and international attention.

Kenneth Lieberthal, Foreign Affairs,
March/April 2005.

President Bush's stance on Taiwan, which appears to be balanced, has several motivations. . . . Besides its strategic location, Taiwan's future is linked to America's credibility. Cutting through diplomatic verbiage, the United States must help defend Taiwan—or see its alliances with South Korea, Japan, the Philippines, Thailand, and Australia crumble. A failure to aid Taiwan would be seen all over Asia as a lack of American resolve and would damage, and possibly destroy, the United States as a power in the Western Pacific.

Then there is domestic politics. The Bush Administration is driven by the slogan ABC—anything but Clinton. The distaste for the policies of President Clinton, including what they see as his soft posture on China is palpable. Hard-line conservatives, critical of any US move that would appear to accommodate China, press Bush from his right.

More long range is American public opinion. The US view of Taiwan has become more favorable as Taiwan has held elections and fashioned a free-market economy. A recent Gallup poll showed that 62 percent of Americans had a favorable image of Taiwan, while 22 percent had an unfavorable view and 16 percent had no opinion. Two years ago, only 47 percent had a favorable view of Taiwan. . . .

Americans, who preach democracy and respect for human rights, cannot abandon a democracy and still retain moral credibility. This is a question of the destiny of 23 million people who want little more than to be left alone to determine their own future as a democracy and market economy. In the maneuvering of heavyweights, the fate of small nations—and their people—should not be overlooked.

> *"China cannot invade Taiwan, even under its most favorable assumptions about how a conflict would unfold."*

War with China over Taiwan Is Unlikely

Michael O'Hanlon

In the following viewpoint Michael O'Hanlon, a visiting lecturer at Princeton and a fellow at the Brookings Institution, a foreign policy research center, argues that China could not hope to successfully invade Taiwan if the island declared its independence. According to O'Hanlon, the Chinese air and sea capabilities could not bring a large enough invasion force to bear on Taiwan's defenses. Any attempt to make air or sea landings would be defeated by easily mobilized Taiwanese defenders. For this reason and the diplomatic troubles such an attack would bring, O'Hanlon does not believe that the Chinese government would attempt to seize the island.

As you read, consider the following questions:

1. In the author's view, why would Taiwan's air force likely survive China's attempts to eliminate it?

2. According to O'Hanlon, how many Taiwanese troops could be repositioned on the island within any given forty-eight-hour period?

Michael O'Hanlon, "Why China Cannot Conquer Taiwan," *International Security*, vol. 25, Fall 2000. Copyright © 2000 by the President and Fellows of Harvard College and the Massachusetts Institute of Technology. Reproduced by permission.

3. What does O'Hanlon list as some of the potential consequences to China and its government if it chose to invade Taiwan?

War over Taiwan could take a number of forms. An attempted PRC [People's Republic of China] invasion of
Taiwan is the most dire possibility.... Some Pentagon analysts believe that China could prevail in such an attack. As a
1999 Department of Defense report puts it, a "campaign would
likely succeed—barring third-party intervention."...

My conclusions suggest strongly, however, that China could
not take Taiwan, even if U.S. combat forces did not intervene
in a conflict. Nor will China be able to invade Taiwan [until]
at least [2010], if not much longer....

Coercive uses of force are more likely than an invasion—
both because their costs to Beijing would be lower, and because their prospects of success would be greater. They include, most notably, a ballistic missile attack or a naval
blockade. In these scenarios, however, the United States would
have time to make any necessary military response; Taiwan's
very survival would not be at immediate risk....

Failure to Cripple Taiwan's Air Power

For China to seize Taiwan, it would probably have to begin by
attacking key assets including airfields, command-and-control
facilities, and ships using its missiles, aircraft, and special
forces. It would hope to do so with surprise, so that Taiwan
could not first relocate its airplanes, get its ships under way,
and begin general military mobilization while its command-
and-control infrastructure was still intact. This tactic would
constitute China's only hope of establishing air and sea dominance, which in turn would represent its only hope of rapidly
deploying enough troops ashore on Taiwan to stand a chance
in subsequent land battles.

After the surprise attack, China would then assemble and load up amphibious and airborne assets to cross the Taiwan Strait en masse. . . .

To carry out a successful surprise attack against key Taiwanese assets, China could not start loading and sailing most of its ships toward Taiwan until the missile and air strikes had begun. In fact, the PRC would do extremely well simply to prepare its air and missile forces for the attack without having those preparations detected by Taiwanese and U.S. intelligence.

Consider first China's large ballistic missile force. These missiles are numerous, perhaps now totaling 200 or more in southeastern China near Taiwan, with the PRC adding an estimated 50 missiles a year there, according to U.S. Pacific Comdr. Adm. Dennis Blair [in a March 8, 2000, *Washington Post* article]. . . . China's ballistic missiles are inaccurate, however. They might achieve an occasional hit on a runway, but the missiles' accuracy—typically no better than 300 meters—would be too poor to make that happen more than every tenth shot or so . . .

Chinese attack aircraft could probably do better. If China could get several hundred of its 800 to 1,000 attack aircraft through to runways, it could render some of them unusable at least temporarily and perhaps destroy part of the Taiwanese combat air fleet on the ground as well. But it is not clear that all or even most of China's attack planes would be available against Taiwan's airfields. Moving the bulk of them to bases near Taiwan could tip off Taipei and Washington about a pending military action, allowing Taiwan's air defenses to be alerted, mines to be laid, and reservists to be mobilized. . . .

Even if its runways were badly damaged . . . Taiwan would be able to keep aircraft in the air. . . . All told, of Taiwan's 600 or so combat aircraft, at least half would likely survive even a well-coordinated, large-scale Chinese preemptive attack that caught Taiwan by surprise. . . .

Luckovich. © by The Washington Post Writers Group. Reproduced by permission.

China's Limited Seaborne Capabilities

China would face several daunting constraints and challenges if it attempted to invade Taiwan by sea. Few PRC troops could deploy over water, given China's very limited amounts of military sealift. Its 70 or so amphibious ships could move no more than 10,000 to 15,000 troops with their equipment, including some 400 armored vehicles (airlift could move another 6,000 troops or perhaps somewhat more counting helicopter transport). These shortfalls would be magnified by China's other military weaknesses. Although Chinese military personnel are generally competent at basic infantry skills, the armed forces do not tend to attract China's best and brightest, nepotism is prevalent, party loyalty is of paramount importance, most soldiers are semiliterate peasants serving short tours of duty, and a strong professional noncommissioned officer corps is lacking. Combined-arms training, although somewhat enhanced of late for elite rapid reaction forces, is infrequent. To quote the Pentagon, "China probably has never conducted a large-scale amphibious exercise which has been fully coordinated with air support and airborne operations."

Taiwan of course has weaknesses of its own, beyond those cited above. It fails to foster cooperation and joint training between the different arms of its military. In addition, Taiwan has not integrated its communications systems to make systematic use of early-warning data and other key information. Among its other, generic military shortcomings, Taiwan continues to rely on conscription to fill out its force structure; thus turnover in the ranks is high, and the quality of the force is limited.

Most of Taiwan's weaknesses are not, however, as severe as China's. Moreover, the basic numbers work strongly in Taiwan's favor. It has a large military of 240,000 active-duty ground troops and 1.5 million more ground-force reservists. With a coastal perimeter of about 1,500 kilometers, Taiwan could deploy roughly 1,000 defenders per kilometer of coastline along all of its shores if it wished. So over any given stretch of 10 to 15 kilometers, a fully mobilized Taiwanese defense force could station as many troops as China could deploy there with all of its amphibious fleet. . . .

So China would be unlikely to establish even a local, temporary advantage along the section of beach where it elected to try coming ashore. . . .

Nor could China subsequently build up its initial force as quickly as Taiwan could strengthen local defenses at the point of attack. In other words, China also lacks the third crucial element of most successful invasions identified above. Whatever happened during the first day of conflict, Taiwan could almost surely deploy large numbers of reinforcements by road on the first night of the war and thereafter. The Chinese air force has limited capacity for finding and attacking mobile ground targets as well as for operating at night, so it could not seriously slow such reinforcements. . . .

China's inability to stop Taiwan's road traffic would have dire consequences for the PRC. Faced with nothing more than Chinese aerial harassment, most of it only during daylight hours, Taiwan could certainly move reinforcements at least 50 kilometers per day. That would make more than 100,000 troops potentially available within forty-eight hours on most parts of the island. . . .

If it somehow established an initial lodgment ashore, China could try to reinforce it using its small amphibious fleet. But China would probably need at least two days for each round-trip of its ships, and even that schedule would be highly contingent on encountering good seas in the notoriously foul-weathered Taiwan Strait. Moreover, returning ships would need to resupply troops already ashore, limiting their ability to deliver reinforcements. After forty-eight hours, therefore, Taiwan would likely have more than 100,000 troops facing the PRC's total of perhaps 20,000 at Beijing's chosen point of attack—and the situation would continue to deteriorate from there for China. . . .

An Airborne Assault Could Not Be Supported

Could China seize a port or an airfield, or both, through an airborne operation? If successful, it would then be able to use commercial airlift and/or sealift to bring in reinforcements as quickly as they could be loaded up, sent across the strait, and unloaded. Reportedly, Taiwan's army has not provided enough protection for ports and airfields, perhaps offering Beijing a glimmer of hope that it could pull off this type of operation.

China has the capacity to airlift about two brigades' worth of paratroopers in a sortie of its entire military airlift fleet. That is possibly enough to establish at least temporary control of both a port and an airfield—but just barely. When seizing such facilities, it is generally considered necessary to control the surrounding area for several miles in each direction to prevent enemy direct-fire weapons from shooting at ships, planes, runways, and piers. Doing so typically requires at least a brigade of troops per facility, according to U.S. military doctrine.

PRC paratroopers (or troop-carrying helicopters) over Taiwan would be at great risk, however, from Taiwan's fighters, SAMs [surface-to-air missiles], and antiaircraft artillery. To mitigate these dangers, China would need to attempt an airborne landing at nearly the same time that it was launching initial attacks against Taiwan's airfields and other key infrastructure—further complicating an already complex opening operation. . . .

Even if China somehow managed tactical surprise with its first sortie of airlift, thus keeping initial losses to a minimum—a highly dubious proposition—it would have only about 6,000 to 8,000 soldiers on the ground as a result. Efforts to reinforce and resupply them would have to cope with alerted Taiwanese air defenses. . . .

Unless Taiwanese SAM batteries and antiaircraft artillery sites were suppressed by Chinese attack aircraft, Taiwan would be able to detect and fire at most airplanes delivering reinforcing troops. And it is doubtful that China could suppress Taiwanese air defenses. The PLAAF [Chinese air force] has mediocre electronic warfare and precision-strike capabilities. It might be able to find large runways and drop unguided bombs on them; it would not be likely to find and jam or destroy smaller, more easily camouflaged antiair weapons. . . .

Implications of a Failed Invasion

China cannot invade Taiwan, even under its most favorable assumptions about how a conflict would unfold. Nor will it be able to do so [until 2010], if not much longer. Its best hope of pulling off a successful invasion would be to first mount a large-scale surprise attack with missiles, air power, and special forces. The PRC would follow up as quickly as possible with an airborne and amphibious assault. Even assuming a rather successful Chinese preemptive attack, however, Taiwan would be able to continue significant flight operations. Taiwan would also retain very effective antiaircraft artillery, surface-to-air missiles, coastal defense guns, coastal patrol craft, and antiship missiles—not to mention a mobilized and large ground army. Taiwan would be able to reinforce its defenses in sectors under intense PRC attack much faster than China could reinforce any initial positions it managed to establish on Taiwan. . . .

In broader political terms, attacking Taiwan would be extraordinarily risky for the ruling regime in Beijing. It would likely lose much of its elite military personnel and a large fraction of its strategic transport capabilities, combat aircraft, and navy in any such attack. A PRC government that attempted such an invasion could fall in its aftermath. . . .

Taipei should hardly be cavalier about moving toward a declaration of independence, however. Even if its military could hold off a full-bore Chinese assault, Taiwan would suffer substantial damage in the process. Blockade and missile-strike scenarios could also cause it great harm. In fact, even a limited blockade effort conducted by China's modest modern submarine force could stand a reasonable chance of dragging down Taiwan's economy—and keeping it down for a prolonged period. U.S. military intervention might be needed to break the blockade quickly.

What are the policy implications of this assessment for Washington? The first is that there is no need to commit to Taiwan's defense in advance. For an invasion scenario—the only one in which China could physically seize Taiwan and present the world community a fait accompli—the United States would not need to participate militarily because Taiwan could defeat China on its own. For other scenarios, U.S. assistance might be required, but it would be less urgent. The United States would have time to react—or to pressure the parties to a diplomatic solution—before feeling the need to intervene militarily itself. In short, the United States should maintain its policy of strategic ambiguity. That desirable policy has helped restrain hard-liners on both sides of the strait historically, and continues to do so today without putting Taiwan at mortal peril.

Periodical Bibliography

The following articles have been selected to supplement the diverse views presented in this chapter.

Thomas Bickford	"Myths and Realities of China's Military Power," *Foreign Policy in Focus*, April 30, 2001.
Pete Engardio, Stan Crock, and Mark L. Clifford	"Sea Change on China," *Business Week*, May 21, 2001.
Bill Gertz	"Chinese Dragon Awakens: Taiwan Seen as Likely Target Within 2 Years," *Washington Times*, June 26, 2005.
Bates Gill and James Mulvenon	"China's Nuclear Agenda," *New York Times*, September 7, 2001.
Ellis Joffe	"The Military Is Transformed: A Slow Process," *International Herald Tribune*, July 16, 2002.
Robert D. Kaplan	"How We Would Fight China:" *Atlantic Monthly*, June 2005.
Anatoly Klimenko	"On the Evolution of China's Military Policy and Military Strategy," *Far Eastern Affairs*, 2004.
Melinda Liu and John Barry	"Soft Power, Hard Choices: China Is Emerging as a Major Economic Power, but Will That Translate into a Military Threat? Taiwan Will Be the Test," *Newsweek*, March 7, 2005.
Richard J. Newman and Kevin Whitelaw	"China: How Big a Threat?" *U.S. News & World Report*, July 23, 2001.
Lijun Sheng	"The Taiwan Issue: Does China Have a Strategy?" *Cambridge Review of International Affairs*, April 2002.
Michael D. Swaine	"Trouble in Taiwan," *Foreign Affairs*, March/April 2004.

OPPOSING
VIEWPOINTS®
SERIES

CHAPTER 4

What Is the State of China's Democratization?

Chapter Preface

China has the largest population on Earth. At 1.3 billion, China's citizenry is about 4.5 times larger than that of the United States. The huge population causes concern for the nation's leaders. Feeding, housing, employing, and finding enough power to supply the needs of so many people is daunting. To ease the burden on the state, the Chinese government passed a "one couple, one child" policy in 1979. Carrying out the policy meant teaching birth control and family planning to the entire nation. Much of the rural population, however, did not adapt to the spirit of the plan. Since male children had more economic opportunities than their female counterparts, reports surfaced that rural parents were committing infanticide to do away with female children born under the one-child law. In response, the government relaxed the rule in the countryside during the late 1980s.

Human rights activists around the globe consider China's initiative to be barbaric. Not only were couples penalized if they had more than one child (and these penalties could include incarceration), but there were allegations that some provincial leaders, who were tasked with implementing the law, compelled women to have abortions for any surplus pregnancies. A 1991 law supplementing the one-child policy even proposed the use of sterilization as a method of keeping the population under control.

In discussing the newly updated 2002 Population and Family Planning Law, Zhao Bingli, vice minister of the State Family Planning Commission, told an interviewer, "After 30 years of efforts, exponential population growth has been effectively controlled, and some 300 million births have been prevented." Bingli and his government colleagues argue that limiting China's birth rate improves the quality of life for the entire population. According to their rationale, fewer children improves health services (fewer patients), allows for better food distribution (more calories per person), and combats unemployment (more available jobs). They even attest that relieving mothers of the trials of repeated pregnancies—especially later in life—gives women more opportunity to participate in economic and social activities. In these respects, China's leaders insist that controlled population growth is essential for building a more liberal nation and one that is responsive to the welfare of the entire populace. In the following chapter defenders and critics of China's internal policies debate whether the nation's leaders are, indeed, improving the welfare of the people or whether their actions bespeak a different agenda.

> "China's overall national strength has risen by a big margin, the people have received more tangible benefits than ever before, and China has enjoyed long-term social stability and solidarity."

The Communist Party Is Promoting Liberal Reform in China

Jiang Zemin

Jiang Zemin served as the general secretary of the Communist Party of China from 1989 to 2002. In the following viewpoint Zemin asserts that the Communist Party has brought the nation to new levels of prosperity and socialist democracy. While the latter cannot be equated to Western democracy, Zemin maintains that in the new millennium the Chinese are more informed of public matters, protected by the rule of law, and allowed greater self-governance in "well-managed" communities.

As you read, consider the following questions:

1. According to Jiang Zemin, how had the standard of living improved for the Chinese people in 2002?

2. What challenges does Jiang say must still be overcome in the new era of Chinese prosperity?

Jiang Zemin, report at the 16th Party Congress of the United Nations, November 17, 2002.

3. Jiang argues that the CPC is extending democracy in China. What examples does he give to show the CPC's commitment to this goal?

As human society entered the 21st century, we started a new phase of development for building a well-off society in an all-round way and speeding up socialist modernization. The international situation is undergoing profound changes. The trends toward world multipolarization and economic globalization are developing amidst twists and turns. Science and technology are advancing rapidly. Competition in overall national strength is becoming increasingly fierce. Given this pressing situation, we must move forward, or we will fall behind. Our Party must stand firm in the forefront of the times and unite with and lead the Chinese people of all ethnic groups in accomplishing the three major historical tasks: to propel the modernization drive, to achieve national reunification and to safeguard world peace and promote common development, and in bringing about the great rejuvenation of the Chinese nation on its road to socialism with Chinese characteristics. This is a grand mission history and the era have entrusted to our Party. . . .

Expanding Markets and Improving Democracy

Reform and opening up have yielded substantial results. The socialist market economy has taken shape initially. The public sector of the economy has expanded and steady progress has been made in the reform of state-owned enterprises. Self-employed or private enterprises and other non-public sectors of the economy have developed fairly fast. The work of building up the market system has been in full swing. The macro-control system has improved constantly. The pace of change in government functions has been quickened. Reform in finance, taxation, banking, distribution, housing, government institutions and other areas has continued to deepen. The open economy has developed swiftly. Trade in commodities and services and capital flow have grown markedly. China's foreign exchange reserves have risen considerably. With its accession to the World Trade Organization (WTO), China has entered a new stage in its opening up.

Notable progress has been registered in improving socialist democracy and spiritual civilization. Continued efforts have been made to improve democracy and the legal system. New steps have been taken in political restructuring. The patriotic united front [the bond between the government and the people] has grown stronger. Further progress has been made in the work relating to ethnic, religious and overseas Chinese affairs. Fresh progress has been made in keeping public order through comprehensive measures. Science, technology, education, culture, health, sports, family planning and other undertakings have moved ahead. The media and publicity work as well as ideological and moral education have kept improving. The people's cultural life has become increasingly rich and colorful.

New strides have been taken in strengthening national defense and army building. Efforts have been redoubled to make the People's Liberation Army more revolutionary, modernized and regularized. Our national defense capabilities and the army's defense and combat effectiveness have further improved. The army, the armed police and the militia have played an important role in defending and building up our motherland.

On the whole, the people have reached a well-off standard of living. The income of urban and rural residents has gone up steadily. The urban and rural markets have been brisk, and there has been an ample supply of goods. The quality of life of the residents has been on the rise, with considerable improvement in food, clothing, housing, transport and daily necessities. There has been marked progress in building the social security system. The seven-year program to help 80 million people out of poverty has been in the main fulfilled.

Fresh progress has been made in the great cause of national reunification. The Chinese Government has resumed the exercise of sovereignty over Macao. The principle of "one country, two systems"[1] has been implemented and the basic laws of Hong Kong and Macao special administrative regions have been carried out to the letter. Hong Kong and Macao enjoy social and economic stability. Personnel, economic and cultural exchanges across the Taiwan Straits have kept increasing. The fight against "Taiwan independence" and other attempts to split the country has been going on in depth.[2]

New Prospects have been opened up in our external work. In light of the developments and changes in the international situation, we have adhered to the correct foreign policy and related principles. We have carried out both bilateral and multilateral diplomatic activities extensively and taken an active part in international exchanges and cooperation. China's international standing has risen still further. . . .

Clean and Responsive Government

An all-out endeavor has been made to build up the Party ideologically, organizationally and in work style. Our ideological and political work has been strengthened. New steps have been taken in the reform of the personnel system. The endeavor to build a clean and honest government and combat corruption has been going on in depth and yielding fresh notable results.

Facts prove that the major policy decisions taken by the Central Committee at and since the Fifteenth National Congress [in 1997] are correct and accord with the fundamental interests of the overwhelming majority of the people. Our

1. the policy aimed at unifying the people of Hong Kong and Macao with mainland China while tolerating these former colonies' foreign systems of government

2. Taiwan insists that it is independent of China, but the Chinese government maintains that it is part of greater China.

The Chinese Ambassador to the UN Defends China's New Leadership

China is now under a new generation of leadership who is inspired by the ideal of building a people-centered government and is committed to do all it can in the interest of the people. Under this government, the Chinese people have successfully overcome the SARS [severe acute respiratory syndrome] epidemic and achieved an annual GDP [gross domestic product] growth rate of 9.1 percent. Given the fact that 900 million out of our 1.3 billion population live in the rural area, this government has given top priority to resolving issues of farm, farming and farmers and has set the target of removing all types of agricultural taxes within five years, and providing health care for migrant workers and education for their children. Today, China's per capita GDP exceeds 1000 US$, while its population in poverty, has reduced from 250 million in 1978 to 29 million [as] of last year [2003]. Average life expectancy of the Chinese has increased from 35 years before the new China was established to 71.4 years . . . today [in 2004]. . . .

China is neither heaven nor hell. China is just in the process of building a society with decent living standards. The Chinese government is confident that it has the capability of gradually solving the problems in the process of its development. All that the Chinese government is doing is to satisfy the Chinese people. As long as they are happy and satisfied, our government will unswervingly continue its work.

Sha Zukang, statement to the United Nations on draft resolution entitled "Human Rights Situation in China," April 15, 2004.

achievements are the outcome of the united endeavor of the whole Party and the people of all ethnic groups of the country. They provide a more solid foundation for the future development of the cause of the Party and state.

We must be clearly aware that there are still quite a few difficulties and problems in our work. The income of farmers and some urban residents has increased only slowly. The number of the unemployed has gone up. Some people are still badly off. Things have yet to be straightened out in the matter of income distribution. The order of the market economy has to be further rectified and standardized. Public order is poor in some places. Formalism, the bureaucratic style of work, falsification, extravagance and waste are still serious problems among some leading cadres in our Party, and corruption is still conspicuous in some places. The Party's way of leadership and governance does not yet entirely meet the requirements of the new situation and new tasks. Some Party organizations are feeble and lax. We must pay close attention to these problems and continue to take effective measures to solve them. . . .

Building Prosperity, Building Socialism

Over the past 13 years [i.e., since 1989], with clearly defined objectives, we worked with one heart and one mind and scored historic achievements. In 2001, China's GDP reached 9.5933 trillion yuan, almost tripling that of 1989, representing an average annual increase of 9.3 percent. China came up to the sixth place in the world in terms of economic aggregate. On the whole, the people made a historic leap from having only adequate food and clothing to leading a well-off life. As is universally recognized, the 13 years have been a period in which China's overall national strength has risen by a big margin, the people have received more tangible benefits than ever before, and China has enjoyed long-term social stability and solidarity and had a good government and a united people. China's influence in the world has grown notably, and the cohesion of the nation has increased remarkably. The hard work of our Party and people and their great achievements have attracted worldwide attention and will surely go down as a glorious page in the annals of the great rejuvenation of the Chinese nation.

A review of these 13 years shows that we have traversed a tortuous course and that our achievements are hard won. We have responded confidently to a series of unexpected international events bearing on China's sovereignty and security. We have surmounted difficulties and risks arising from the political and economic spheres and from nature. We have gone through one trial after another and removed all kinds of obstacles, thus ensuring that our reform, opening up and modernization drive have been forging ahead in the correct direction like a ship braving surging waves. We have attained these successes by relying on the correct guidance of the Party's basic theory, line and program, on the high degree of unity and solidarity of the Party and on the tenacious work of the whole Party and the people of all ethnic groups around the country. . . .

In building socialism with Chinese characteristics, the fundamental interests of the people of the whole country are identical, on the basis of which concrete interest relations and internal contradictions can be adjusted. In the formulation and implementation of the Party's principles and policies, a basic point of departure is that we should represent the fundamental interests of the overwhelming majority of the people, and correctly reflect and take into account the interests of different groups of people, enabling the whole people to advance steadily toward the goal of common prosperity. We should protect the vitality for further growth of the developed regions, strong industries and people who have become rich first through hard work and lawful business operations and encouraging them to create social wealth. More importantly, we must pay great attention to less developed areas and the industries and people in straitened circumstances and show concern for them. In particular, we must see to it that the people in financial difficulties have subsistence allowances, and we must take effective measures to help them find jobs and improve their living conditions so that they will truly feel the warmth of our socialist society. . . .

Extending Democracy

Extending democracy at the grassroots level is the groundwork for developing socialist democracy. We will improve grassroots self-governing organizations, their democratic management system and the system of keeping the public informed of matters being handled, and ensure that the people directly exercise their democratic rights according to law, manage grassroots public affairs and programs for public good and exercise democratic supervision over the cadres. We will improve self-governance among villagers and foster a mechanism of their self-governance full of vitality under the leadership of village Party organizations. We will improve self-governance among urban residents and build new-type and well-managed communities featuring civility and harmony. We will uphold and improve the system of workers' conferences and other democratic management systems in enterprises and institutions and protect the legitimate rights and interests of workers. . . .

We must see to it that there are laws to go by, the laws are observed and strictly enforced, and law-breakers are prosecuted. To adapt to the new situation characterized by the development of a socialist market economy, all-round social progress and China's accession to the WTO, we will strengthen legislation and improve its quality and will have formulated a socialist system of laws with Chinese characteristics by the year 2010. We must see to it that all people are equal before the law. We should tighten supervision over law enforcement, promote the exercise of administrative functions according to law, safeguard judicial justice and raise the level of law enforcement so that laws are strictly implemented. We must safeguard the uniformity and sanctity of the legal system and prevent or overcome local and departmental protectionism. We will extend and standardize legal services and provide effective legal aid. We should give more publicity to the legal system so that the people are better educated in law. In particular, we will enhance the public servants' awareness of law and their ability to perform their official duties according to law. Party members and cadres, especially leading cadres, should play an exemplary role in abiding by the Constitution and other laws. . . .

The CPC [Communist Party of China] is deeply rooted in the Chinese nation. Since the very day of its founding, it has been the vanguard of the Chinese working class and also of the Chinese people and the Chinese nation, shouldering the grand mission of realizing the great rejuvenation of the Chinese nation. During the new-democratic revolution, our Party united and led the Chinese people of all ethnic groups in fulfilling the historic task of winning national independence and people's liberation, thus laying the groundwork for our great national rejuvenation. After the founding of New China [in 1949 when the Communists took control], our Party creatively completed the transition from New Democracy to socialism, the greatest and most profound social transformation ever in China's history, and embarked on a socialist road and the historical journey to the great rejuvenation of the Chinese nation. . . . Our Party has found the correct road to socialism with Chinese characteristics, injecting new and greater vitality into our drive for national rejuvenation. Splendid prospects present themselves before the great cause of rejuvenation of the Chinese nation.

"Rising prosperity, especially in the cities. . ., does seem to be buying off or diverting potential pressures for democratic political change."

The Communist Party Is Thwarting Liberal Reform in China

Jacques deLisle

In the following viewpoint Jacques deLisle argues that the democracy movement in China has lost its momentum in large part because the government has substituted economic progress for democratic reform. However, deLisle maintains, this strategy—convincing the Chinese people that material prosperity is the key to improving their lives—will fail if the economy falters. In that case, he maintains, the Communist Party will likely use its age-old methods of authoritarian control. DeLisle, a law professor at the University of Pennsylvania, is director of the Asia Program of the Foreign Policy Research Institute.

As you read, consider the following questions:

1. What two reasons does deLisle claim explain why the Chinese government may not be able to equate economic prosperity with democratic reform for long?

Jacques deLisle, "Fifteen Years After Tiananmen: Persistence, Memory, and Change in China," www.fpri.org, June 4, 2004. Copyright © 2004 by the Foreign Policy Research Institute. Reproduced by permission.

2. According to the author, what did the Communist Party do on the eve of the fifteenth anniversary of the Tiananmen incident?

3. In deLisle's view, what are three examples of reform-minded "civil society" sprouting up in China in the new millennium?

On the eve of June 4, 1989, a statue dubbed the "Goddess of Democracy" stood opposite Mao's giant portrait at Tiananmen Square, until the forces of the People's Liberation Army [PLA] brought it crashing down during an infamous night of brutality and bloodshed in the Chinese capital. Although the fifteenth anniversary of those events has been uneventful, the Goddess of Democracy still haunts the Chinese leadership that lives and works in a compound just down the main avenue from where the participants in the student-led Democracy Movement had erected the statue and exposed reform-era China's potential for producing severe popular discontent and organized, regime-shaking opposition. At the same time, the issues and passions that energized the popular movement symbolized by the statue seem a distant and faded memory in a city where the streets leading to the square are jammed with foreign-brand cars and ablaze with neon signs hawking a cornucopia of consumer goods and services. These are garish testaments to China's seeming ability to make breathtaking market-based economic growth and resilient authoritarian politics coexist smoothly and, perhaps, symbiotically. A decade and a half after the Tiananmen Incident, the paradox of Tiananmen's seemingly long shadow and apparent irrelevance characterizes China in almost every major area of politics and policy. . . .

Pushing Economics over Political Change

Fifteen years after Tiananmen, the overwhelmingly dominant story in China is, and has long been, economics, not politics.

And that economic story is, of course, one of astoundingly rapid and transformative (though unevenly distributed) change. In the dozen years since preeminent leader Deng Xiaoping's famous "southern tour" [in 1992] relaunched the economic reform agenda after its post-Tiananmen lull, the city where the Tiananmen Incident occurred and, even more so, other metropolises farther south along China's coast and, in aggregate statistics at least, China as a whole, have reached levels of prosperity, urbanization, industrialization, post-industrialization and linkage to the outside world that far exceed anything seen or, perhaps, even much imagined in 1989. As a result, a sizable and increasingly cosmopolitan and property-owning middle class—and a narrower stratum of truly rich—have emerged.

The question raised, at least obliquely, by the Democracy Movement of 1989—the relationship between economic development and political democracy in reform-era China—remains unanswered in 2004. For the time being, the reform-era leadership's long-standing strategy appears to be holding: Rising prosperity, especially in the cities (whence challenges to the existing order typically have arisen in almost everywhere in the world except, ironically, China), does seem to be buying off or diverting potential pressures for democratic political change. Market-based economic prosperity and the absence of political democracy cohabitate more comfortably in China circa June 4, 2004 than they did circa June 4, 1989.

Still, there are reasons to doubt the long-term stability of this arrangement a decade and a half after the Tiananmen demonstrations seemed to imperil it. First, although opinion is divided, many reputable analyses of China's economy foresee the possibility that the economic ingredient in the formula for prosperity and stability could prove very hard to sustain in the relatively near future. . . .

Second, at a macro-level, the global correlation between market-based prosperous economies and human rights-protecting democratic polities (especially in countries of substantial size, and at least where markets have been in place for some time) remains strikingly strong. Similarly, the venerable assertion that a large middle class increases pressure for broadened participation in politics and governance seems to have a good deal of validity. . . .

Maintaining Authoritarian Rule

Perhaps the clearest meaning of the events of June 4, 1989, was that the Chinese Communist Party leadership was, in the end, deeply determined to preserve authoritarian rule (and the order it maintained), even if that required paying dearly in citizens' lives, regime legitimacy and (it seemed plausible at the time) economic growth. Fifteen years later, the agenda of the 1989 Democracy Movement has made little headway, and many aspects of the authoritarian politics of the 1980s appear to remain remarkably intact despite the many changes that have swept China. But this political pattern has been sustained only with considerable effort and cost by a regime that remains wary and worried that the popular political forces on display at Tiananmen a decade and a half ago could resurface. There may be some truth to the arguments from critics (or optimists) at home and abroad that the events around June 4, 1989, struck a devastating and still potentially fatal blow to the regime.

Many signs point to the lack of political change. The type of democracy that the students on the square and their intellectual patrons and sources of inspiration advocated has not developed. Village elections, with roots predating Tiananmen, have been slow to grow, generally extend only to very basic-level units, and fall far short of the levels of contestation, autonomous participation and openness contemplated by relatively robust definitions of democracy. . . . Although in many ways political discussion has become much freer in China since 1989, the heady "democracy salons" of the pre-

Tiananmen years have not returned. Jiang Zemin—who rose to become Deng's heir [in 1989] in part because he kept the potentially disruptive democracy movement in Shanghai under control in 1989—lingers as a powerful political figure. Despite his nominal retirement [in 2002], the most prominent beneficiary of the Tiananmen crackdown remains as head of the commission overseeing the military. [He retired from that post in 2004.] His proteges pack the current Politburo [the Chinese congress] and constrain China's new top two leaders, Hu Jintao and Wen Jiabao. Inner-party democracy, although much touted in recent years, is an old idea with pre-Tiananmen origins. And it is still a far cry from political democracy in the ordinary sense.

The regime's apparent success in securing the basic political status quo does not, however, seem secure, confident or effortless. . . .

A would-be Democracy Party and other forms of organized political dissent have been routinely and thoroughly suppressed. So too was Falun Gong [a religious meditation sect], once the regime recognized its organizational prowess and its growing (if reactive or defensive) political tinge. On the eve of the fifteenth anniversary of the Tiananmen Incident, the authorities predictably detained the usual suspects, including prominent non-exiled dissidents, and also the PLA doctor whose exposure of the SARS [severe acute respiratory syndrome] problem in Beijing had only a year earlier made him a folk hero for the new openness and a prominent voice advocating political reforms.

The pervasive corruption that was among the complaints of students and ordinary citizens in 1989 persists (albeit in an evolved form) and remains a source of popular discontent and regime delegitimation, prompting a seemingly endless and only modestly successful series of anti-corruption drives mandated by the highest levels of the Party and state.

Democracy Discarded

Deng Xiaoping's death in 1997 . . . marked a new phase in the party's search for legitimacy. "Democracy" as an official political aspiration could not quite yet be discarded, but the party now insisted that the Chinese were too ill-educated to be able to exercise it properly. . . .

Nowadays, the whole idea of democracy is mocked. Western democracy is criticised for its hypocrisy, and non-western democracy for risking destructive populism, a disorder supposedly rampant in Taiwan and threatening stability in Hong Kong. In so far as it still mentions democracy at all, the Communist Party restricts it to "the work of selecting and appointing cadres" within its own ranks, with a few experiments in strictly controlled elections to party offices in selected cities. . . .

Thus, . . . since 1989, the Communist Party has gone full circle, from making compromises under the pressure of a worldwide wave of democratisation, back to rising proudly above that discourse, and reclaiming its absolute rule over both the national government and all levels of local government.

Wang Chaohua, New Statesman,
January 1, 2005.

Uncertain Signs of Change

On the other hand, persisting authoritarianism has not meant political stasis. In Beijing and in other cities in 2004, there are indications aplenty of political change and possible harbingers of a more fundamental political transformation. Ordinary citizens' freedom and willingness to think and say unorthodox and highly critical things have become assumed and accepted, no longer having the risky novelty that they did in the later 1980s.

The regime's and leadership's tolerance for (and interest in) ideas for significant political reforms arguably have become more well-established than they were when Zhao Ziyang and Deng Xiaoping invited and patronized such discussions in the 1980s. The Hu Jintao/Wen Jiabao leadership has placed new and unprecedented emphasis on government openness and accountability, particularly in the aftermath of officials' disastrous attempts to cover up SARS. . . .

Possible sprouts of civil society can be found in many places, including within a few miles of Tiananmen Square. Among the many examples are: NGO's [nongovernmental organizations] and citizens' groups focusing on environmental issues; organized protests and sustained movements by about-to-be-displaced residents seeking to slow or prevent urban redevelopment; and middle and upper class homeowners' associations determined to hold real estate developers and city officials to their promises concerning open space and other amenities.

Most of these current signs of political change and the social and economic underpinnings for them are primarily phenomena of the relatively elite and affluent urban sector, much as the Democracy Movement of 1989 had been. Then, as now, major and lasting political change in China will have to involve other, larger segments of the populace as well. . . .

Keeping the Masses Quiescent

Today, many outside observers, Chinese commentators, and Party leaders alike recognize that the greatest threat to stability and regime continuity in China stems from the hundreds of millions of Chinese who have been left behind in the country's reform-era rush to riches. Where once economic development (which often meant little more than high GDP [gross domestic product] growth rates) was the unquestioned preeminent goal, relatively mainstream sources now speak of the need to attend equally to the needs of "social development." Discontent at deprivation—both relative and absolute—percolates among the residents of the inland areas where foreign investment lags and linkages to the global economy are few. The farmers face declining social services, heavy and arbitrary tax burdens, eroding terms of trade (all the more so with the WTO's mandate to open Chinese markets to food imports), and disproportionately little access to the wealth associated with the rise of industrial and service sectors. Workers in China's rust-belt state industries whose factories are closing or shedding workers amid painful restructuring are unable to compete with newer collective, private and foreign firms. Finally, a vast and growing underclass of rural to urban migrants fill the cities' insecure and low-paying factory, domestic, construction and day-labor jobs. . . .

For now at least, keeping the long-neglected masses quiescent seems to depend relatively little on strategies of active cooptation, or substantial near-term amelioration of their condition, or incorporation of their preferences through prodemocratic processes. Instead, it depends on old familiar methods. It depends on satisfying the continued popular desire for rising prosperity and the high degree of order that the Party has been able to provide and that many Chinese today see the 1989 protesters as having recklessly endangered. It also depends on the Party's and state's continuing effective monopoly over organized politics—a monopoly that was badly rattled at Tiananmen fifteen years ago and that the leadership has striven relentlessly to rebuild and maintain ever since.

"Authorities continued to use provisions of the Criminal Law relating to 'subversion', 'state secrets' and other vaguely defined national security offences to prosecute peaceful activists and advocates of reform."

China Still Suffers from Human Rights Abuses

Amnesty International

Amnesty International (AI), a worldwide human rights watchdog organization, issues an annual "State of the World's Human Rights" report that identifies what the organization believes are ongoing human rights violations in various nations. In the following viewpoint, a selection from the 2005 report, AI indicts China for human rights abuses. Included in the charges are the Chinese government's lax public health policies; its use of torture, prolonged detention, and the death penalty in dealing with dissidents; and its suppression of human rights advocates. Such abuses continue, the organization claims, despite the Chinese government's avowal to institute new legal reforms and protections.

As you read, consider the following questions:

1. According to Amnesty International, what human rights

violation is the Chinese government carrying out in preparation for the 2008 Olympics in Beijing?

2. For what crime does AI claim the Chinese government authorities sentenced Kong Youping, a member of the Chinese Democratic Party, to prison for fifteen years?

3. Under what pretext are Chinese authorities unjustly making arrests in the Uighur community, in the authors' view?

The new administration [in the People's Republic of China], which had taken office in March 2003, consolidated its authority, particularly following the resignation of former president Jiang Zemin as chair of the Central Military Commission in September [2002]. Some legal reforms were introduced, including new regulations aimed at preventing torture in police custody and an amendment to the Constitution in March stating that "the state respects and protects human rights." However, the failure to introduce necessary institutional reforms severely compromised the enforcement of these measures in practice.

The authorities took a more proactive approach towards dealing with China's HIV/AIDS epidemic, including a new law in August [2004] aimed at strengthening AIDS prevention and stopping discrimination against those living with AIDS or other infectious diseases. However, grassroots activists campaigning for better treatment continued to be arbitrarily detained.

Political crackdowns continued on specific groups, including the Falun Gong spiritual movement, unofficial Christian groups, and so-called "separatists" and "religious extremists" in Xinjiang and Tibet.

The authorities continued to engage in "human rights dialogue" with other countries, but suspended their dialogue with the USA after the latter proposed a resolution on China at the UN Commission on Human Rights in March [2004]. . . .

Silencing Human Rights Champions

The authorities continued to use provisions of the Criminal Law relating to "subversion", "state secrets" and other vaguely defined national security offences to prosecute peaceful activists and advocates of reform. Lawyers, journalists, HIV/AIDS activists and housing rights advocates were among those harassed, detained or imprisoned for documenting human rights abuses, campaigning for reform, or attempting to obtain redress for victims of violations.

Ding Zilin, who set up the "Tiananmen Mothers" group to campaign for justice following the killing of her son in Beijing on 4 June 1989 [when students demonstrated in a pro-democracy rally], was detained by the police in March [2004] to prevent her from highlighting her concerns. She was also placed under a form of house arrest a few days before the 15th anniversary of the crackdown to prevent her from filing a legal complaint on behalf of 126 others who also lost relatives in 1989.

Li Dan, an AIDS activist, was detained by police in Henan province in August [2004] in an apparent attempt to prevent him from protesting against the government's handling of the AIDS epidemic. He was released one day later but then beaten up by two unknown assailants. Li Dan had founded a school for AIDS orphans in the province where up to one million people are believed to have become HIV-positive after selling their blood plasma to unsanitary, state-sanctioned blood collection stations. The school had been closed down by the local authorities in July.

Forced Evictions

The rights of freedom of expression and association of workers' representatives continued to be severely curtailed and independent trade unions remained illegal. In the context of economic restructuring, large numbers of people were reportedly denied adequate reparations for forcible eviction, land requisition and job layoffs. Public and largely peaceful protests against such practices increased, leading to numerous detentions and other abuses.

Beijing was often the focus for such protests due in part to house demolitions during the city's preparations for the Olympics in 2008. People also travelled to Beijing from other parts of the country to petition the central authorities after failing to obtain redress at the local level. Tens of thousands of petitioners were reportedly detained by Beijing police during security operations in advance of official meetings in March and September [2004].

Ye Guozhu was detained on suspicion of "disturbing social order" in August after applying for permission to hold a mass protest against forced evictions in Beijing. He was sentenced to four years in prison in December. Ye Guozhu and his family had been forcibly evicted from their home in Beijing last year [2004] to make way for construction reportedly related to the 2008 Olympics.

Violence Against Women

Numerous articles about domestic violence appeared in the national media, reflecting widespread concern that such abuses were not being effectively addressed.

Serious violations against women and girls continued to be reported as a result of the enforcement of the family planning policy, including forced abortions and sterilizations. In July the authorities publicly reinforced a ban on the selective abortion of female foetuses in an attempt to reverse a growing gap in the boy-girl birth ratio.

Women in detention, including large numbers of Falun Gong practitioners, remained at risk of torture, including rape and sexual abuse.

New regulations were introduced in January [2004] preventing the police from issuing on-the-spot fines to prostitutes. However, "Custody and Education" continued to be used to detain alleged prostitutes and their clients without charge or trial.

Mao Hengfeng was sent to a labour camp for 18 months' "Re-education through Labour" in April [2004] for persistently petitioning the authorities over a forced abortion 15 years earlier when she became pregnant in violation of China's family planning policy. She was reportedly tied up, suspended from the ceiling and severely beaten in the labour camp. She had been detained several times in the past in psychiatric units where she had been forced to undergo shock therapy.

Repressing Political Activists

Political activists, including supporters of banned political groups, or those calling for political change or greater democracy continued to be arbitrarily detained and in some cases sentenced and imprisoned. By the end of the year, AI had records of more than 50 people who had been detained or imprisoned after accessing or circulating politically sensitive information on the Internet.

Kong Youping, a leading member of the Chinese Democratic Party and former union activist in Liaoning province, was sentenced to 15 years' imprisonment in September [2004] for "subversion". He had been detained in late 2003 after posting articles on the Internet attacking official corruption and urging a reassessment of the 1989 pro-democracy movement.

Repressing Spiritual and Religious Groups

The Falun Gong spiritual movement remained a key target of repression, which reportedly included many arbitrary detentions. Most of those detained were assigned to periods of "Re-education through Labour" without charge or trial, during which they were at high risk of torture or ill-treatment, particularly if they refused to renounce their beliefs. Others were held in prisons and psychiatric hospitals. According to over-

Breen. © 2000 by Asbury Park Press. Reproduced by permission.

seas Falun Gong sources, more than 1,000 people detained in connection with the Falun Gong had died since the organization was banned in 1999, mostly as a result of torture or ill-treatment.

Other so-called "heretical organizations" and unofficial religious groups were also targeted. Reports increased of arrests and detentions of unregistered Catholics and members of unofficial Protestant "house churches". Those attempting to document such violations and send reports overseas were also at risk of arrest.

Zhang Shengqi, Xu Yonghai and Liu Fenggang, three independent Protestant activists, were sentenced to one, two and three years in prison respectively by the Hangzhou Intermediate People's Court for "leaking state secrets" in August [2004]. The charges related to passing information abroad about crackdowns on Protestants and the closure of unofficial churches in the area.

The Death Penalty

The death penalty continued to be used extensively and arbitrarily, at times as a result of political interference. People were executed for non-violent crimes such as tax fraud and embezzlement as well as drug offences and violent crimes. The authorities continued to keep national statistics on death sentences and executions secret. Based on public reports available, AI estimated that at least 3,400 people had been executed and at least 6,000 sentenced to death by the end of [2004] although the true figures were believed to be much higher. In March [2004], a senior member of the National People's Congress announced that China executes around 10,000 people per year.

A lack of basic safeguards protecting the rights of defendants meant that large numbers of people continued to be sentenced to death and executed after unfair trials. In October [2004] the authorities announced an intention to reinstate Supreme Court review of death penalty cases and to introduce other legal reforms aimed at safeguarding the rights of criminal suspects and defendants. It remained unclear, however, when these measures would be introduced. . . .

Torture, Arbitrary Detention, and Unfair Trials

Torture and ill-treatment continued to be reported in a wide variety of state institutions despite the introduction of several new regulations aimed at curbing the practice. Common methods included kicking, beating, electric shocks, suspension by the arms, shackling in painful positions, and sleep and food deprivation. Political interference in the rule of law, restricted access to the outside world for detainees, and a failure to establish effective mechanisms for complaint and investigation continued to be key factors allowing the practice to flourish.

The authorities officially announced an intention to reform "Re-education through Labour", a system of administrative detention used to detain hundreds of thousands of people for up to four years without charge or trial. However, the exact nature and scope of reform remained unclear.

People accused of political or criminal offences continued to be denied due process. Detainees' access to lawyers and family members continued to be severely restricted and trials fell far short of international fair trial standards. . . .

Crackdowns in the Xinjiang Uighur Autonomous Region

The authorities continued to use the "global war on terror" to justify harsh repression in Xinjiang, resulting in serious human rights violations against the ethnic Uighur community [a Muslim people]. The authorities continued to make little distinction between acts of violence and acts of passive resistance. Repression resulted in the closure of unofficial mosques, arrests of imams, restrictions on the use of the Uighur language and the banning of certain Uighur books and journals.

Arrests of so-called "separatists, terrorists and religious extremists" continued and thousands of political prisoners, including prisoners of conscience, remained in prison. Many of those charged with "separatist" or "terrorist" offences were reportedly sentenced to death and executed. Uighur activists attempting to pass information abroad about the extent of the crackdown were at risk of arbitrary detention and imprisonment. . . .

No Improvements in the Tibet Autonomous Region

Freedom of religion, expression and association continued to be severely restricted and arbitrary arrests and unfair trials continued. Over 100 Tibetan prisoners of conscience, mainly Buddhist monks and nuns, remained in prison. Contacts between the Chinese authorities and representatives of the Tibetan government in exile continued, with some signs that progress was being made. However, this failed to result in any significant policy changes leading to improved protection for the basic human rights of Tibetans.

Topden and Dzokar, two monks from Chogri Monastery, Drakgo (Luhuo) County, Sichuan province, together with Lobsang Tsering, a layman, were all reportedly sentenced to three years in prison in August [2004] for putting up posters advocating Tibetan independence. They had been detained in July together with numerous others who were released several days later. Some said they were beaten in detention.

"In 2004, the [National People's Congress] Standing Committee examined drafts of 33 laws. . . and adopted 25 of them, providing further legal guarantee for economic and social development and human rights."

China Is Making Advances in Human Rights

Information Office of the State Council of the People's Republic of China

In April 2005 China's Information Office of the State Council issued a government white paper entitled China's Progress in Human Rights in 2004. According to the white paper, excerpted in the following viewpoint, the Chinese government is doing much to improve the rights of the citizenry. The government argues that it is ensuring due process of law by fighting to clean up corruption among public officials and police forces and by making it easier for the people to have access to fair and impartial legal justice. In addition, other human rights abuses—including lengthy imprisonment and the torturing of criminal suspects—are being cleared up, as supervision of local officials is heightened.

As you read, consider the following questions:

1. According to the white paper, the creation of what new

Information Office of the State Council of the People's Republic of China, China's Progress in Human Rights in 2004, www.china.org.cn, April 2005.

institutions raised the level of village self-government in the Chinese countryside?

2. As mentioned in the white paper, what aspects of religious conduct does the government document entitled "Regulations on Religious Affairs" regulate?

3. The white paper maintains that public security organs examined 1,871 laws and regulations pertaining to the rights and duties of civilians, legal persons, and organizations. What was the fate of the majority of these laws?

In 2004, China adhered to the road of political development with Chinese characteristics. It actively promoted democracy in political affairs and the building of political civilization to guarantee the citizens' civil and political rights.

The National People's Congress (NPC) and the local people's congresses at various levels are the organs through which the people exercise state power. The NPC and its Standing Committee are playing a more and more important role in governing the country according to law and guaranteeing the people's democratic rights. The amendments to the Constitution adopted at the Second Session of the Tenth NPC in 2004 added many new provisions to the Constitution that are closely related to human rights. In 2004, the NPC Standing Committee examined drafts of 33 laws, interpretations of laws and decisions related to legal issues, and adopted 25 of them, providing further legal guarantee for economic and social development and human rights. Of them, the amended Law of Election of the NPC and Local People's Congresses further improved the election system, standardized the election procedures, and expanded and guaranteed the citizens' right of election. The amendments made to the law on the prevention and treatment of epidemics focused on the prevention of and early warning on epidemics, strengthened control over the spread of epidemics and medical treatment measures, and provided greater guarantee for the rights of citizens, sufferers from infectious diseases, and actual and suspected virus carriers. The recently adopted decision on the improvement of the system of people's jurors increased the transparency of the activities of the judicial departments, strengthened citizens' supervision over such activities and provided a guarantee for the procedural rights of citizens. . . .

Building Democracy

The building of grass-roots democracy in the countryside entered a new phase. In 2004, the State Council issued the "Opinions on Making Village Affairs Public and Improving the Democratic Management System," which helped improve the system of making village affairs public and the system of democratic management at the grass-roots level and promote protection of ordinary villagers' democratic rights. A democratic management system based on the "Regulations on Villagers' Self-government" and "Village Regulations and Agreements" was established all over the country. A democratic decision-making system mainly in the form of villagers' congresses and representative conferences, and a democratic supervision system based on making village affairs public and democratic evaluation were also established, thus considerably raising the level of villagers' self-government within the framework of the law. A campaign was launched to create "exemplary villages of democratic management and rule of law." At present, about 10 percent of villages across the country have been awarded this honor.

The state pays special attention to guaranteeing—through petitions and visits—citizens' right to criticize, make suggestions, appeal to higher authorities, file a charge and report an offence. In 2004, the State Council revised the "Regulations on Petitions and Visits." The revised edition increased the government's responsibilities by demanding that its powers and responsibilities should be balanced, and highlighted the principles that all matters concerning petitions and visits should be conducted in an open manner and be convenient for the people, and the citizens' rights and interests must be protected. In 2004, the state created a joint meeting system to solve the most difficult problems encountered when handling petitions and visits, and cases involving large numbers of people, with focus being put on problems caused by house demolition, relocation in towns and cities, and requisition of land in the countryside, and intensified its supervision on the handling and solution of the problems. . . .

Free Speech, Workers' Rights, and Religious Freedom

Citizens' freedom of information, of speech and of the press is protected by law. At present, a three-level news briefing system consisting of the State Council's Information Office, and various departments of the State Council and provincial governments has basically been established. Sixty-two departments of the State Council have established the news briefing system, and appointed 75 spokespersons. Twenty-three provinces (autonomous regions and municipalities directly under the central government) have established the news briefing system, and 20 of them have appointed spokespersons. Last year [2004], 44 departments of the State Council gave some 270 news conferences, and 28 provinces (autonomous regions and municipalities directly under the central government) gave 460 news conferences. These activities greatly increased the transparency of government work, and helped citizens become better informed about administrative affairs. Protection of citizens' rights to information, supervision and participation in public affairs were further promoted. In 2004, the state enacted a series of laws and regulations to further improve China's press system and ensure that citizens can better exercise their right of freedom of the press.

Employees' right to participate in and organize trade unions has been further exercised and developed. In 2004, a national check was conducted of the enforcement of the "Trade Union Law," which promoted the building of trade union organizations. Special efforts were made to establish trade unions in non-public enterprises and have migrant workers join trade unions. The year 2004 also saw a considerable development of grass-roots trade union organizations and trade union members. By the end of September 2004, China had 1.02 million grass-roots trade union organizations, 115,000 more than in the previous year, an increase of 12.6 percent. . . .

Citizens enjoy the freedom of religious belief in accordance with law. Religious groups, venues for religious activities, the legitimate rights and interests of religious adherents and their normal religious activities are protected by law. In 2004, the State Council promulgated China's first comprehensive administrative regulation on religious matters—"Regulations on Religious Affairs." It clearly defines the rights of religious groups and adherents with regards to religious activities, establishment of religious colleges and schools, publishing of religious books and periodicals, management of religious properties and foreign religious exchanges. It also regulates the administrative acts of relevant departments of the government so as to ensure that the legitimate rights and interests of religious believers, religious groups and venues for religious activities are not infringed upon. According to incomplete statistics, China has now more than 100 million religious adherents, more than 100,000 venues for religious activities, and about 300,000 clergy members. Normal religious ceremonies or rituals conducted by ministers and all other normal religious activities—carried out either in venues for religious activities or homes of religious adherents in accordance with religious tradition—are taken care of by believers themselves and protected by law. . . .

China Critiques America's Human Rights Record

The United States claims to be "a paragon of democracy," but American democracy is manipulated by the rich and malpractices are common.

The United States is the only country in the world that rules out ex-inmates' right to vote, which disenfranchises 5 million ex-inmates and 13 percent [of] male black people.

The 2004 US presidential election reported many problems, including counting errors, machine malfunctions, registration confusion, legal uncertainty, and lack of respect for voters. . . .

The US freedom of the press is filled with hypocrisy. Power and intimidation hang over the halo of press freedom. The *New York Times* published a commentary on March 30, 2004, saying that the US government's reliance on slandering had reached an unprecedented level in contemporary American political history, and the government prepared to abuse power at any moment to threat[en] potential critics. . . .

Human Rights Record of the US in 2004, *Government of the People's Republic of China white paper, April 2005.*

Judicial Reform

In 2004, China strengthened its judicial reform to ensure strict law enforcement and fair administration of justice, and guarantee citizens' legal rights according to law.

China has cracked down on various criminal offences in accordance with law to protect citizens' life and the safety of their property. From January to October 2004, the Chinese public security organs investigated and cracked 2.004 million criminal cases. The people's courts at all levels wound up 644,248 criminal cases of first instance, in which 767,951 criminals were sentenced, effectively protecting the victims' legitimate rights and interests.

Adhering to the principle of "enforcing law in the interest of the people," the public security organs strengthened construction of the law enforcement system to ensure that law enforcement is strict, just and humane, improved the system of supervision over law enforcement, and made real efforts to solve some outstanding problems in law enforcement. From September 2003 to October 2004, the public security organs sorted out all the public security rules and regulations in effect since the founding of the People's Republic of China concerning the rights and duties of citizens, legal persons and other organizations. Among the 1,871 laws and regulations, 558 remained, 1,077 were abolished and 164 amended....

The judicial organs have adopted vigorous measures to prevent and contain extended detention. In 2004, the Chinese procuratorial organs [legal representatives of the state] had no extended detention, and urged other law-enforcing organs to correct the extended detention of 7,132 people. The Chinese courts cleared up 873 old and new cases of extended detention involving 2,432 people, settling all the cases save a handful due to technical legal problems. By the end of 2004, the Chinese public security organs had no extended detention.

Reforming Law Enforcement

The procuratorial organs have performed their functions honestly, conscientiously strengthened legal supervision and safeguarded justice in law enforcement. In 2004, the procuratorial organs rejected applications for the arrest of 67,904 people; supervised over the canceling of investigation of 2,699 cases, which they found should not have been put on file for investigation; made decisions not to prosecute 21,225 people; appealed against court judgments of 3,063 criminal cases and 13,218 civil cases; proposed for review of 4,333 cases; put 5,569 criminal appeal cases on file for reinvestigation and changed the original judgments in 786 cases; and filed for investigation cases of power abuse, dereliction of duty, soliciting or accepting bribes and malpractices for personal gain involving 3,010 judicial personnel, thus effectively safeguarding the citizens' rights and ensuring fairness and justice. . . .

Since May 2004, the Supreme People's Procuratorate has carried out a special campaign to severely deal with criminal cases involving government functionaries' infringement upon human rights by misusing their powers, focusing on cases of illegal detention and search, extorting confessions by torture, gathering evidence with violence, abusing people in custody, disrupting elections as well as serious cases of dereliction of duty that cause heavy losses of life and property of the people. In total, 1,595 government functionaries suspected of criminal activities were investigated and prosecuted, thus effectively bringing under control offences of infringement on rights. . . .

Safeguarding Legal Interests

The trial system with Chinese characteristics has been further improved. Courts at all levels have further carried out the principle of open trial, striving to realize openness in filing for investigation, court hearing, conclusion of trial, and judgment documents and process of enforcement in the hope to promote justice with openness. Observance of trials by the general public has been facilitated with bulletins before trials and simplified procedures for attending trials. Over 50 million citizens observed trials in 2004. . . .

The legal rights and interests of people in custody are protected by law. In 2004, the Ministry of Public Security and the Supreme People's Procuratorate jointly planned, organized and launched a drive to build "model units for strengthening the enforcement of surveillance and legal supervision, and for guaranteeing smooth criminal proceedings and the legal rights and interests of detainees" in all the detention houses throughout China. Consequently, a large number of model detention houses have emerged with advanced facilities, standard law enforcement and humane management. The system of meeting public procurators has been generally established in detention houses, supervision over food, health care and epidemic prevention for detainees has been strengthened, the detainees' physical health and protection of their property has been accorded with greater attention, and the system of informing detainees of their rights, the system of open procuratorial work and visit system have been improved, thus effectively protecting detainees' legal rights and interests.

"When will the ruthless surveillance of writers stop, including that of Wang Yiliang and Liao Yiwu, who have spent years in labor camps and prison cells for daring to write?"

China Lacks Media Freedom

Bei Ling and Andrea Huss

In the following viewpoint Bei Ling and Andrea Huss contend that China's warming relations with the West do not mean that its society is liberalizing. In fact, they argue, China continues to lack media freedom. Publishing or broadcasting unwelcome views can lead to imprisonment, the authors claim. Most media outlets, they maintain, distribute only "approved" news items rather than confront the tyranny of the state. Bei Ling, a Chinese poet and essayist arrested in 2000 for publishing an illegal journal, now lives in America, where he serves on the executive board of the International Center for Writing and Translation at the University of California–Irvine. Andrea Huss is professor of Chinese literature at Wellesley College outside of Boston.

As you read, consider the following questions:

1. What do Ling and Huss claim is the "ticket to a prosperous life" in China?
2. According to the authors, what did literary critic Liu

Xiaobo receive in response to his persistent calls for media reform in China?

3. In Ling and Huss's view, why does the United States have an interest in promoting media freedom in China?

It's the 11th day of the Lunar New Year Festival in China. The money god has been welcomed back to earth with firecrackers, children ride their new bicycles on the roads and back alleyways of Beijing, the Summer Palace is seeing the last of its holiday visitors and all seems right with the world that is China.

In the northwestern corner of the capital city, in a neighborhood that boasts two of China's top universities, Beijing and Qinghua, streets once walked by the greatest intellectuals and revolutionaries in modern Chinese history are now home to information technology moguls. Skyscrapers loom large, luxury apartments sell for $2,000 a square meter, and businessmen send their children to school in well waxed, coal black Audi A6's. The head of China's most popular and successful English institute, the New Oriental School, Yu Minhong, can barely keep up with the ranks of students wrangling to secure space in his classes. Entry into the World Trade Organization [in 2001] has given China new and much deserved confidence. Good English skills are the ticket to a prosperous life. Talent need no longer make its way abroad to find success. There is a confidence in individual ability, a sense of promise, hope and freedom unprecedented in post-1949 Chinese life [i.e., after the People's Republic was founded].

There is much to be thankful for in this new year of the horse [2002]. There is also much that should not be forgotten. As President [George W.] Bush addressed students at Qinghua University in Beijing on the 30th anniversary of Richard M. Nixon's momentous trip to China [in 1972], where was the mention of the six Qinghua graduate students recently sentenced in southern China's Xiangzhou District Court, in Zhuhai City, for "utilizing an evil cult to sabotage legal enforce-ment"? All are practitioners of Falun Gong, the outlawed meditation movement that numbers its followers in the tens of thousands. They had been writing articles about the perse-cution of Falun Gong members. A confident [then-]President Jiang Zemin claims that these young men and women were arrested for breaking Chinese law, not for their religious be-liefs or for publishing their articles. It was a slippery answer to a complex and painful question: What exactly does freedom of expression mean?

Sharing Democracy?

As Chinese citizens around the country gathered before their TV screens to hear Mr. Bush's speech, we should recall that not far south of the Qinghua campus one of China's most prominent dissidents, the literary critic Liu Xiaobo, has been calling for the reform of China's news media for years now. His appeals have not always fallen on deaf ears: they brought him three years of re-education in a labor camp. Such a sen-tence requires no trial, one of the many quirks in a legal sys-tem responsible for a fifth of the world's population.

As Liu Xiaobo noted in a recent public letter, the fact that China can view a press conference or a presidential address on television does not prove that journalism is free and open. President Jiang's turns on the dance floor with [First Lady] Laura Bush and [then–national security adviser, now secretary of state] Condoleezza Rice at Thursday evening's presidential dinner and his stage-rocking rendition of "O Sole Mio" do not a democratic president make.

Appearances are deceiving. President Bush's visit to Qing-hua came before classes resumed, to a campus of closed doors and pulled curtains. Each audience member, each representa-tive student was carefully chosen, each question censored, a performance orchestrated for an audience whose vision has become blurred by the skyscrapers, the sitcoms preaching the

Censorship on the Internet

An international protest campaign secured the freedom of Chinese blogger [a person who uses Internet Web logs (blogs) as a chat forum] Liu Di, a 23-year-old psychology student who offended authorities with her satirical comments about the Communist Party. Yet, even as Di was released, two individuals who had circulated online petitions on her behalf were arrested. Such is life in China, where an estimated 300,000 bloggers (out of 80 million regular Internet users) uneasily coexist with the government. Bloggers in China have perfected the art of self-censorship, because a single offensive post can affect an entire online community—as when Internet censors temporarily shut down leading blog sites such as Blogcn.com in 2003. Frank Yu, a Program Manager at Microsoft Research Asia's Advanced Technology Center in Beijing, described this mind-set as he profiled a day in the life of a fictional Chinese blogger he dubbed "John X": "After reading over his new posting, he checks it for any politically sensitive terms which may cause the government to block his site. . . . Although he is not concerned as much about being shut down, he does not want all the writers that share the host server with him to get locked out as well. Living in China, we learn to pick the battles that we feel strongly about and let the host of other indignities pass through quiet compliance." Text messaging is a much safer medium for the online Chinese community. Some bloggers, however, do manage to push the envelope, as when Shanghai-based Microsoft employee Wang Jianshuo offered candid, firsthand accounts (including photos) of the SARS and Avian Flu outbreaks.

Daniel W. Drezner and Henry Farrell, Foreign Policy,
November/December 2004.

power of love and money, the European cars, the McDonalds, the Starbucks, the Louis Vuitton bags and sparkling Chanel fragrance counters found in upscale shops around the country.

The United States is at yet another crossroads in its relationship with China. Thirty years have passed. China is experiencing unprecedented prosperity as the United States struggles through a period of painful contemplation. There is much to be remembered, more to be learned. As globalization brings us closer together and as technology beams the smiling faces of two presidents around the world, we should not forget to ask the questions that still need to be asked. When will the media in China be privatized? When will newspaper editors in China be free to publish articles on topics of their choice? When will the ruthless surveillance of writers stop, including that of Wang Yiliang and Liao Yiwu, who have spent years in labor camps and prison cells for daring to write? When will China's people be able to savor and explore the fullest meaning of that phrase, "freedom of expression"?

The U.S. Interest in Free Media

A Chinese government official claimed before Mr. Bush's visit that several political prisoners would be released after the visit. Is this part of the hype that usually surrounds the visits of foreign dignitaries? Yesterday, as the American president's trip wound down, several dozen Christians were arrested in Beijing for gathering together in public. Will jailed dissidents like Xu Wenli, the former chairman of the China Democratic Party who has spent 15 of the last 20 years in jail, finally see the light of day?

We must not become too enthralled with an image of a modern, prosperous China. Americans also must not get lost in the rhetoric of war on terrorism to such a degree that Chinese "cooperation" on that front will blind us to reality. For its own sake, the United States needs to look more closely at its

China policy—and at how this policy is being presented by Chinese news outlets and viewed by the Chinese people. In a country without media freedom, American democracy and power, with some spin, can easily be presented as a hateful American hegemony. Freedom of expression in China is very much in America's interests, in part because without it the government will be able to shape decisively what the Chinese people think of the United States.

On a perfectly beautiful, sunny day in September of 2001, the world was reminded of the price paid for freedom [when terrorists destroyed the World Trade Center and damaged the Pentagon]. Who knew? The sky was clear. The markets were up. The subways were packed with commuters. On this day of the lunar New Year with spring just around the corner, Beijing's Avenue of Heavenly Peace throngs with the last of holiday revelers. The highways are crowded with evidence of new wealth. Customers at a Starbucks in Shanghai pay $3 for a caffe mocha and never feel the sting. And there are writers in prison simply because they are writers. Printing a commentary piece like this could bring a death sentence in China. The sun shone as President Bush's motorcade made its way through Beijing's burgeoning streets, but looks can be deceiving.

| "The role of the Chinese press has changed from a [Chinese Communist Party] propaganda conduit to a provider of news for emerging middle-class consumers."

China's Media Freedom Is Increasing

James Borton

China's media are still state supervised, maintains James Borton in the following viewpoint. However, he argues, many media outlets now function as commercial enterprises due to increased commercialization and reduced state funding. In addition, Borton claims, competition is engendering a higher standard of investigative journalism and leading journalists to pursue a wider range of subject matter, occasionally broaching some politically sensitive topics. According to Borton, the variety of media outlets—including the vast array of Internet news sources—is increasing news circulation and leaving the public hungry for more information. Borton, a freelance journalist, writes extensively on Asian affairs.

As you read, consider the following questions:

1. According to Ashley Esarey, as cited by Borton, how do *Caijing*'s editors stay ahead of the censors?

James Borton, "Free Market Generates (Some) Media Freedom," *Asia Times Online,* July 21, 2004. Copyright © 2004 by Asia Times Online Co. Ltd. All rights reserved. Reproduced by permission.

2. According to Borton, what percentage of Chinese households watch televised news?

3. What news topic did *Caijing* run a cover story on in
2003 when the magazine's journalists noticed discrepan-
cies in a government report, according to the author?

China's free-market economy is generating unprecedented
but not unlimited press freedoms, and there's momentum. As Beijing embraces a market economy, its proliferating
news media too are becoming privatized, more commercial,
combative and fiercely competitive. This gives rise to some of
the best investigative journalism that truly sheds light and
serves the people, and some of the worst sensationalism.

A More Activist Role

Hu Shuli, the crusading editor of *Caijing* magazine, China's
high-profile, successful business publication, recently returned
from Qatar, where she joined 120 Middle Eastern and Western
journalists in a program called "Changing Media Perceptions:
Professionalism and Cultural Diversity." There was plenty of
jousting, as well as thoughtful discussion and debate on the
media's role, duties and responsibilities. The issue of the role
of media has gained traction in the past few years, sparked by
the globalization of information reflected in the emergence of
"new" media. And China, where the media used to be totally
subservient, has taken on a more activist role.

With increased deadlines, the twice-monthly publication
Caijing (the name means "finance and business") is soon to
become a newsweekly, in which young breathless staffers, including two foreigners, write their articles and fact-check in
preparation for the next issue. They work in untidy cubicles,
in the same Beijing office building as Dow Jones.

Caijing and other Chinese media understand all too well
that the development of the country's media industry is not a

smooth process. Political policy fluctuations and cycles of repression and censorship have been the norm over the past two decades.

Never mind, China watchers know that with the rapid shift to a market economy, the Middle Kingdom's[1] state-owned enterprises have been stained with almost inevitable corruption and scandal. No wonder the peripatetic editor has gleefully remarked, "In China there is more news than journalists." *Caijing*'s crusade against corruption and its unstinting journalistic enterprise has netted Hu the moniker, "the most dangerous woman in China." (Repeated efforts to interview Hu were unsuccessful, as her staff said she was too busy.)

Commercialization

The central government's decentralization policies have dictated that the news media commercialize, since state subsidies have been dramatically curbed. The resulting news-media privatization and commercialization have forced China's information gatekeepers to distinguish themselves from keen competition. A proliferation of news media has brought higher standards of compelling reporting in the form of investigative articles, exposes of environmental degradation and also has yielded, at the other end of the spectrum, some of the worst offenses in sensational media coverage, reminiscent of British, US and other tabloids.

Some of these media developments were examined by Ashley Esarey, PhD candidate in the political science department at Columbia University, who interviewed scores of Chinese publishers and journalists. His research confirms that one of the major results of China's decentralization policies is an explosion in the number of news media, in the value of media advertising revenues, in competition for advertising revenue, and in newly found freedom of media companies to report the news—as opposed to party propaganda pablum.

1. a literal translation of Zhongguo—what the Chinese call their country

Considerable Freedom of Expression

Today, the Chinese people can talk freely in private gatherings and even openly in professional meetings without fear of being prosecuted. For instance, a Chinese economics professor openly criticized the labor theory of value (a basic doctrine in Marxian economics) in a paper presented before a conference in Beijing in 1999. There is considerable freedom of the press as the non-government press has expanded rapidly in recent years and attracted a large readership. This includes daily or weekly newspapers, magazines and books. Opinions expressed therein are open and free, subject to only a minor degree of censorship. Censorship of foreign books is almost non-existent. Information available to the public is somewhat restricted because the government has control over TV and radio stations and even the Internet. However, the control is limited because the Chinese have access to short-wave radios and it is difficult to control the use of fax machines and the flow of information through the Internet. People residing near Hong Kong can get access to TV stations in Hong Kong, which are mainly private.

Gregory C. Chow,
Knowing China, *2004.*

"*Caijing* is well known for relatively objective reporting on key events in China,—not merely for economic reporting." Esarey said in a recent online interview with *Asia Times Online.*"Its editors are successful because they stay ahead of censors by printing stories that are off the Propaganda Department's radar screen. They have a strong sense of professionalism and an obligation to report the news, but not at any cost. Because the magazine is a profitable commercial venture, its operators want to remain viable and therefore must follow the explicit wishes of the [Communist] Party concerning content." . . .

China's media policy shapers are caught in a quandary in the ongoing dialogue that somehow permits new media and conventional media to report critically on business abuses, for example, and no longer adopt the [Chinese state newspaper] *People's Daily* propaganda reporting model. For *Caijing* this relaxation of media guidelines has translated into a paid circulation base of more than 85,000 readers. This is a remarkable achievement given that the magazine's newsstand price remains at a premium of US$1 a copy, while the average annual income for a farmer remains around $100 and that of an urban resident the equivalent of $1,000 a year.

"In the past, the Chinese media were either official or semi-official; however, today market-driven media have become China's fastest-growing information sources, as well as some of the more prosperous companies," editor Hu said of the media's role, in a speech to the China Business Summit in Shanghai [in 2003].

The Chinese news media are the official voice of the Chinese Communist Party (CCP), transmitting its political will to the people. Ninety-eight percent of Chinese households, or almost 1.167 billion Chinese out of a total 1.3 billion, watch broadcasts beamed by more than 1,600 television stations. Millions more read 2,137 daily and weekly newspapers.

New Political Reforms Mean Bolder Journalism

With the Middle Kingdom's political landscape ushering in even newer reforms, the media seem to be willing to take bolder actions, which sometimes place editors and reporters in jail or under house arrest at the very least. The questions remain: Are the laws and policies securely in place to allow China's new media to continue their march toward independence, adopt stringent investigative-reporting standards and offer critical commentary? Can China's new news media create a public debate and present options for resolving the country's pressing social, economic and political problems? To what extent are ethical and professional standards being pursued and taught at China's journalism programs?

In the 1980s, leader Deng Xiaoping's motto, "seek truth from facts," set the tone for all kinds of reportage. [In 2004] lively discourse among Beijing's policy shapers has become intense because of the changing communication environment in China. The advent of new technologies and media convergence are generating new opportunities for people to get more connected in the information society. Press systems are opening up, allowing for more creativity, more choices and access to information critical to the demands of development. This was evident [in 2003] in China during the SARS (severe acute respiratory syndrome) outbreak and in the response of the online Chinese media and brazen bloggers.

The media were very tightly controlled in China during the SARS epidemic until mid-April 2003 when *Caijing* found a discrepancy between the information on the epidemic released by the World Health Organization (WHO) and the central government. (This revelation came after *Time* magazine's article on the SARS victims hidden in Beijing military hospitals.) *Caijing* gambled successfully that the CCP could not continue to suppress news on the epidemic once it got on the Internet, and it decided to prepare the cover story "The Beijing files," claims communications Professor Joseph Chan from Chinese University in Hong Kong.

Few dispute that *Caijing* is a pioneer in professional journalism and is a model for emulation, generating new competition. According to a newly released policy white paper commissioned by the International Committee of American Business Media, Chinese authorities have closed down almost 700 periodicals because of new policy shifts, ending "command subscriptions" and transferring party control to publishing companies.

Despite the considerable restrictions on the news media, the role of the Chinese press has changed from a CCP propaganda conduit to a provider of news for emerging middle-class consumers. Even Chinese web portals have encouraged competition among news organizations. News often appears on the Internet either exclusively or before it is disseminated by mainstream traditional print and broadcast media. . . .

Pushing the Envelope

While publishing and other media may still be considered ideologically sensitive, some enterprising Chinese publishers know that a pragmatic brand of self-censorship (knowing how far to push the envelope), coupled with major media initiatives, proliferating media and morphing communication technology, may very well set them free for a short march to commercial growth and press liberalization.

"The [Chinese] Government tries to control and regulate religious groups to prevent the rise of groups that could constitute sources of authority outside of the control of the Government."

China Lacks Religious Freedom

U.S. Department of State

The Bureau of Democracy, Human Rights, and Labor is one of four bureaus that compose the Office of the Under Secretary for Global Affairs (a branch of the U.S. Department of State). In the following viewpoint the bureau reports on the lack of religious freedom in China. China has displayed some tolerance for religious practices within its borders, the authors claim, but only within the confines of state-sanctioned and state-monitored churches. Those who prefer to avoid state scrutiny, the authors argue, are forced to worship in underground churches that the state brands illegal. Members of these underground churches are regularly harassed and subject to criminal prosecution for their disloyalty to the state, the authors maintain.

As you read, consider the following questions:

1. What are China's five officially sanctioned religions, according to the U.S. State Department report?

U.S. Department of State, Bureau of Democracy, Human Rights, and Labor, *International Religious Freedom Report 2004,* www.state.gov, September 15, 2004.

2. What does the report say is the official religion of the Communist Party in China?

3. According to the U.S. State Department report, for how long can cult leaders and recruiters be sentenced to jail?

4. In the U.S. State Department's view, why are there no Vatican representatives in China's sanctioned Catholic Church?

The [Chinese] Constitution provides for freedom of religious belief and the freedom not to believe; however, the Government seeks to restrict religious practice to government-sanctioned organizations and registered places of worship and to control the growth and scope of activities of religious groups. The Government tries to control and regulate religious groups to prevent the rise of groups that could constitute sources of authority outside of the control of the Government and the Chinese Communist Party (CCP). Despite these efforts at government control, membership in many faiths is growing rapidly.

Government Repression

During the period covered by this report, the Government's respect for freedom of religion and freedom of conscience remained poor, especially for many unregistered religious groups and spiritual movements such as the Falun Gong. The extent of religious freedom varied widely within the country. Unregistered religious groups continued to experience varying degrees of official interference and harassment. Members of some unregistered religious groups, including Protestant and Catholic groups, were subjected to restrictions, including intimidation, harassment, and detention. In some localities, "underground" religious leaders reported ongoing pressure either to register with the State Administration for Religious Activities (SARA, formerly known as the central Religious Affairs Bureau) or its provincial and local offices, still known as Religious Affairs Bureaus (RAB). They also reported facing pressure to be affiliated with and supervised by official party organizations linked to the legally recognized churches. For example, some local officials in Henan Province often mistreated unregistered Protestants, and some local officials in Hebei Province tightly controlled Catholics loyal to the Vatican. In other localities, however, officials worked closely with registered and unregistered Buddhist, Muslim, Catholic, and Protestant groups to accomplish religious and social goals. During the period covered by this report, Government officials cautioned against "foreign infiltration under the guise of religion." The Government increased scrutiny of contacts between some citizens and foreigners involved in religion and detained some citizens for providing religious information to foreigners. . . .

Senior government officials claim that the country has no restrictions against minors practicing religious beliefs. In many areas of the country, children are able to participate in religious life with their parents but local officials in some areas forbid children from full religious participation. For example, local officials in Xinjiang Uighur Autonomous Region (Xinjiang) have stated that persons younger than 18 are forbidden from entering mosques in Xinjiang. Local officials in Jilin City also have stated that it is illegal for minors of any faith to participate in religious activities; however, Jilin provincial officials disagree, stating that minors in the province are accorded full religious freedom. Senior government officials have consistently declined to clarify publicly the country's policy toward minors and religion.

The Government continued its repression of groups that it categorized as "cults" in general and of the Falun Gong in particular. The arrest, detention, and imprisonment of Falun Gong practitioners continued. Practitioners who refuse to recant their beliefs are sometimes subjected to harsh treatment in prisons and reeducation-through-labor camps and there have been credible reports of deaths due to torture and abuse. Christian-based groups that the Government considered cults were subjected to increased government scrutiny during the period covered by this report.

The communities of the five official religions—Buddhism, Islam, Taoism, Catholicism, and Protestantism—coexist without significant friction; however, in some parts of the country relations between registered and unregistered Christian churches are tense.

The U.S. Government discusses religious freedom issues with the Government as part of its overall policy to promote human rights. President [George W.] Bush discussed religious freedom during his December 2003 meeting with Premier Wen Jiabao. Senior U.S. officials called on the Government to halt the abusive treatment of religious adherents and respect religious freedom. Since 1999, the Secretary of State has designated China a "Country of Particular Concern" under the International Religious Freedom Act for particularly severe violations of religious freedom. The Department of State, the U.S. Embassy in Beijing, and the U.S. Consulates General in Chengdu, Guangzhou, Shanghai, and Shenyang made concerted efforts to encourage religious freedom. In Washington and in Beijing, in public and in private, U.S. officials repeatedly urged the Government to respect citizens' constitutional and internationally recognized rights to exercise religious freedom and to release all those serving sentences for religious activities. U.S. officials protested the imprisonment of and asked for further information about numerous individual religious prisoners. During the period covered by this report, some religious prisoners were released from prison, including Tibetan nun Phuntsog Nyidrol.[1]

1. Phuntsog Nyidrol, first arrested in October 1989 for taking part in peaceful demonstrations, was sentenced to nine years imprisonment. Her sentence was extended to seventeen years when she, along with other nuns, secretly recorded a cassette of songs praising the Dalai Lama and calling for an independent Tibet, which was smuggled out of prison.

The Law and Religion

The Criminal Law states that Government officials who deprive citizens of religious freedom may, in serious cases, be sentenced to up to 2 years in prison; however, there were no known cases of persons being punished under this statute.

The State reserves to itself the right to register and thus to allow particular religious groups and spiritual movements to operate. For each of the five officially recognized religions, there is a government-affiliated association that monitors and supervises its activities. The State Council's State Administration for Religious Activities (SARA) is responsible for monitoring and judging the legitimacy of religious activity. The SARA and the CCP United Front Work Department (UFWD) provide policy "guidance and supervision" on the implementation of government regulations regarding religious activity, including the role of foreigners in religious activity. Employees of SARA and the UFWD are rarely religious adherents and often are party members. Communist Party members are directed by party doctrine to be atheists.

Chinese law requires religious groups to register places of worship. Spiritual activities in churches that have not registered may be considered illegal and participants can be punished. . . .

Some groups register voluntarily, some register under pressure, and the authorities refuse to register others. Some religious groups have declined to register out of principled opposition to state control of religion. Others do not register due to fear of adverse consequences if they reveal, as required, the names and addresses of church leaders. Unregistered groups also frequently refuse to register for fear that doing so would require theological compromises, curtail doctrinal freedom, or allow government authorities to control sermon content. Some groups claimed that authorities refused them registration without explanation or detained group members who met with officials to attempt to register. The Government contended that these refusals mainly were the result of these groups' lack of adequate facilities.

The Government has banned all groups that it has determined to be "cults," including the Falun Gong and the Zhong Gong movements (Zhong Gong is a qigong exercise discipline with some mystical tenets.) After the revised Criminal Law came into effect in 1997, offenses related to membership in unapproved cults and religious groups were classified as crimes of disturbing the social order.

Local Restrictions and Harassment

Government sensitivity to Muslim communities varied widely. In some predominantly Muslim areas where ethnic unrest has occurred, especially in Xinjiang among the Uighurs, officials continued to restrict or tightly control religious expression and teaching. Police cracked down on Muslim religious activity and places of worship accused by the Government of supporting separatism. . . .

During the period covered by this report, local officials destroyed several unregistered places of worship around the country, although there were no reports of the widespread razing of churches. In Zhejiang Province, for example, there were reports that a few churches and hundreds of shrines were destroyed in the period from July to October 2003. Zhejiang authorities often claimed that destroyed buildings were not zoned for religious activities and [were] thus unsafe. . . .

Some local authorities continued a selective crackdown on unregistered churches, temples, and mosques, and the Central Government failed to stop these activities. Police closed underground mosques, temples, and seminaries, as well as some Catholic churches and Protestant "house churches," many with significant memberships, properties, financial resources, and networks. Several unregistered church leaders reported continuing pressure from local authorities. Despite these efforts at control, official sources, religious professionals, and members

The Fate of One Chinese Pastor and His Family

[In September 2004] the pastor of [an underground Protestant] church, Cai Zhuohua, was arrested. Police from China's Security Bureau searched his home and a neighboring building that housed a printing press. The owners of the press had cooperated with Cai to print some 230,000 Bibles and religious tracts. The police confiscated all of these materials and arrested two young women who were working at the press. They were later released, but remain under watch.

Cai's wife, who was not with her husband at the time of his arrest, fled to a coastal province, but was caught shortly thereafter. Her older brother and his wife were also arrested. They, along with Cai, are still being held incommunicado. The only members of the pastor's immediate family to avoid arrest were his four-year-old son and his 70-year-old mother.

Jason Lee Steorts, National Review,
January 31, 2005.

of both officially sanctioned and underground places of worship all reported that the number of religious adherents in the country continued to grow. . . .

Cults

In 1999, the Standing Committee of the National People's Congress adopted a decision, under Article 300 of the Criminal Law, to ban all groups the Government determined to be "cults," including the Falun Gong. The Supreme People's Court and the Supreme People's Procuratorate also provided legal directives on applying the existing criminal law to the Falun Gong. The law, as applied following these actions, specifies prison terms of 3 to 7 years for "cult" members who "disrupt public order" or distribute publications. Under the law, "cult" leaders and recruiters may be sentenced to 7 years or more in prison.

During the period covered by this report, government repression of the Falun Gong spiritual movement continued. At the National People's Congress session in March, Premier Wen Jiabao's Government Work Report emphasized that the Government would "expand and deepen its battle against cults," including Falun Gong. Thousands of individuals were still undergoing criminal, administrative, and extrajudicial punishment for engaging in Falun Gong practices, admitting that they adhered to the teachings of Falun Gong, or refusing to criticize the organization or its founder. There were credible reports of torture and deaths in custody of Falun Gong practitioners....

Catholics and Muslims

In 1999, the Party's Central Committee issued a document directing the authorities to tighten control over the official Catholic Church and to eliminate the underground Catholic Church if it did not bend to government control. There has been continued pressure by the Chinese Catholic Patriotic Association on underground Catholic bishops to join the official Church, and the authorities have reorganized dioceses without consulting church leaders. The Government has not established diplomatic relations with the Holy See [the Vatican], and there is no Vatican representative on the Mainland. The Government's refusal to allow the official Catholic Church to recognize the authority of the Papacy in many fundamental matters of faith and morals has led many Catholics to reject joining the official Catholic Church on the grounds that this denies one of the foundational tenets of their faith....

There are large Muslim populations in many areas, but government sensitivity to these communities varied widely.

Generally speaking, the country's Hui [mixed-ethnicity Chinese] Muslims, who often live in Han [pure-blood] Chinese communities throughout the country, have greater religious freedom than Turkic Muslims such as the Uighurs, who are concentrated in the western part of the country. In areas where ethnic unrest has occurred, especially among the Uighurs in Xinjiang, officials continued to restrict the building of mosques and the training of clergy and prohibited the teaching of Islam to children. In addition to the restrictions on practicing religion placed on party members and government officials throughout the country, in Xinjiang teachers, professors, and university students are not allowed to practice religion openly. However, in other areas, particularly in areas populated by the Hui ethnic group, there was substantial mosque construction and renovation, and also apparent freedom to worship. . . .

Detentions and Abuse of Practitioners

According to Falun Gong practitioners in the United States, since 1999 more than 100,000 practitioners have been detained for engaging in Falun Gong practices, admitting that they adhere to the teachings of Falun Gong, or refusing to criticize the organization or its founder. The organization reports that its members have been subject to excessive force, abuse, detention, and torture, and that some of its members have died in custody. For example, in December 2003, Falun Gong practitioner Liu Chengjun died after reportedly being abused in custody in Jilin Province. Foreign observers estimate that half of the 250,000 officially recorded inmates in the country's reeducation-through-labor camps are Falun Gong adherents. Falun Gong places the number even higher. Hundreds of Falun Gong adherents were also incarcerated in legal education centers, a form of administrative detention, upon completion of their reeducation-through-labor sentences. According to the Falun Gong, hundreds of its practitioners have been confined to psychiatric institutions and forced to take medications or undergo electric shock treatment against their will. During April to June 2003, official Chinese media accused Falun Gong adherents of "undermining anti-SARS operations." Over 180 Falun Gong adherents were detained for allegedly inciting public panic and "spreading false rumors about SARS."

In April [2003], dozens of members of the Three Grades of Servants Church, which the Government labels a "cult," were detained in Heilongjiang Province. Gu Xianggao, allegedly a church member, was beaten to death in a Heilongjiang Province security facility shortly after these detentions. Public security officials paid compensation to Gu's family for the death.

In some areas, security authorities used threats, demolition of unregistered property, extortion, interrogation, detention, and at times beatings and torture to harass leaders of unauthorized groups and their followers. Unregistered religious groups that preach beliefs outside the bounds of officially approved doctrine (such as imminent coming of the Apocalypse or holy war) or groups that have charismatic leaders often are singled out for particularly severe harassment. Some observers have attributed the unorthodox beliefs of some of these groups to poorly trained clergy and lack of access to religious texts. Others believe that some individuals may be exploiting the reemergence of interest in religion for personal gain.

Many religious leaders and adherents have been detained, arrested, or sentenced to prison terms. Local authorities also use an administrative process to punish members of unregistered religious groups. Citizens may be sentenced by a nonjudicial panel of police and local authorities to up to 3 years in reeducation-through-labor camps. Many religious detainees and prisoners were held in such facilities during the period covered by this report.

"The fact is that the citizens' right to religious freedom has been respected and guaranteed in accordance with law."

China Safeguards Religious Freedom

Chinese Embassy in the United States

In the following viewpoint released in America through the Chinese embassy, a Chinese state news source recounts how Dong Yunhu, a state functionary, rebutted the conclusions drawn by the Commission on International Religious Freedom in its 2003 report. Yunhu argued that freedom of religion is protected by law in China. He claims, however, that lawbreakers—regardless of their religious affiliation—are subject to criminal prosecution, and that the Falun Gong cultists are being brought before the courts for these crimes and not for their religious outlook.

As you read, consider the following questions:

1. According to the authors, on what did the U.S. commission base its inaccurate findings?
2. The authors mention that freedom of religion should not be used to further what three unsettling objectives?
3. What event do the authors use as evidence that the U.S. government abuses freedom of religion to counter threats to the state?

Embassy of the People's Republic of China in the United States, "Signed Article Rebuts Report on China's Religious Freedom," www.china-embassy.org, May 23, 2003.

Dong Yunhu, vice-chairman and secretary-general of the China Society for the Study of Human Rights, reprimanded on May 23 [2003] a distorted report by the United States on China's religious freedom.

In his signed article, Dong noted that the 2003 Report of the United States Commission on International Religious Freedom (USCIRF) released on May 13 [2003] the fourth annual report of the commission, again passed itself off as the "Judge of the World's Human Rights," hoisting "the banner of safeguarding religious freedom" while hurling false accusations against religious freedom in developing countries.

In the section on China's religious situation, the report, basing its arguments on hearsay and surmise, listed China among the "countries of particular concern" and willfully distorted the situation with its freedom on religious belief and cited the country as a "particularly severe violator of religious freedom."

This reckless distortion has misled the international community, smeared China's reputation and, once again betrayed the scheme of some forces in the United States which have the sinister motive of using human rights and religious issues to oppose China, said the article.

Religion Is Protected by Law

For instance, the report claims that China's protection of religious freedom has been deteriorating during the current reporting year [2003]. However, the fact is that the citizens' right to religious freedom has been respected and guaranteed in accordance with law.

The Chinese Constitution specifies that the citizens in China enjoy full freedom in religious belief and that no administrative organs, institutions or individuals can force or forbid conversion to a certain religion, and discrimination either among adherents of a faith or between the religious

An Astounding Number of Religious Adherents in China

The best demographers tell us that there are certainly over 50 million and possibly as high as 70 million [Christians in China]. If that is the case, then China represents the single greatest indigenous growth of evangelical Christianity in the history of the church. When the missionaries were forced out in 1948, the best estimates were that there were between 2 million and 2.5 million evangelicals in China. If the conservative figure of 50 million is true, that is incredible growth. If it is 90 million, it is hardly fathomable. The official report from the government is that there are 100 million believers in China. That is everybody—Buddhist, Taoist, Christians, whatever. We know that figure is very, very conservative.

Don Argue, "Report on Religious Freedom in China," speech delivered at the International Coalition for Religious Freedom Conference on Religious Freedom and the New Millennium, Tokyo, Japan, May 23–25, 1998.

people and atheists, is prohibited.

In addition, the legitimate interests of religious groups conducting lawful activities are to be protected by the government.

Since the launch of its opening-up and reform policies in the late 1970s, China has made gigantic advances in the maintenance of political stability, economic growth, social progress and national unity, which has created a favorable environment for the improvement of the cause of Human Rights and Religious Freedom, said the article.

Incomplete official statistics show that there are more than 100 million religious adherents in China and over 85,000 sites for religious activities. With more than 3,000 religious groups, the country has some 300,000 religious personnel.

China has entered a golden era in terms of the guarantee of human rights, and the Chinese are, as any unbiased people may see, enjoying their religious freedom in an unprecedented way, said the article.

No Prisoners of Conscience

By ignoring the hard, objective facts and maliciously vilifying China's image, the report has an ulterior motive, it [the article] said.

The report also deliberately defiles China by alleging that "the Chinese government discriminates against individuals on the basis of their religion or belief" and that "Chinese continue to be confined, tortured, imprisoned, and subject to other forms of ill treatment on account of their religion or belief."

However, noted the article, the fact is that China is a country governed by the rule of law, which means that all citizens are equal before the law, irrespective of religious affiliation or belief, and no one will be brought to justice unless he or she has violated Chinese laws.

There have been precisely no cases of people practicing normal religious activities being jailed or sentenced, and the so-called "prisoners of conscience" described in the report do not exist in China at all, said the article.

Referring to the cases cited by the report to prove its sensational argument, the article said that the sentences were imposed on some people wholly due to their criminal offenses, and it had nothing to do with their belief in religions.

According to the principle of "All Chinese Citizens Are Equal before the Law," all people in China, including the religious people and atheists, enjoy equal rights and civic responsibilities according to law, and no one is permitted to conduct illegal activities in the name of religion.

Given that this is a common practice in any country governed by the rule of law, it's rather ridiculous to see that the report had portrayed China as a "severe violator of religious freedom," said the article.

American prisons are home to more than 2 million inmates, most of whom are religious believers of different kinds. In accordance with the logic of the report then, the article queried, can the United States be deemed as the severest violator of religious freedom?

Worship Responsibly

It is known to all that the constitutional rights and responsibilities go hand in hand. Chinese laws grant citizens the right of religious freedom, but also stipulate the responsibilities they have to carry out, namely, that no one should utilize any religion to undermine social stability, cause injury to the physical and mental health of the people or constitute an obstacle to the country's educational system.

This is in basic compliance with the International Covenant on Civil and Political Rights, which also says that the free expression of religion or belief must not undermine social security, social order, public health, ethics or other people's basic rights and freedoms, said the article.

Therefore, it's rather groundless and unjust for the report to label the Chinese government's advocacy for lawful restrictions against religious activities to protect "social security, social order and public health," as an "infringement upon religious freedom," said the article.

As the report spoke openly and positively of the insidious Falun Gong cult, the article noted that it allows the world to once again see through the dual standards set by the United States on human rights issues.

Insidious cults have been identified as a public hazard worldwide, and it is a common practice for many countries to uproot evil cults to protect their people's lives, security and assets, and to guarantee the normal activities of different religions, as well as their religious freedom.

In February 1993, the Federal Investigation Bureau of the United States launched a massive assault on an evil cult compound in Waco, Texas, which was created by David Koresh.

After a tear gas and artillery attack that lasted 51 days, more than 80 people were killed in the battle fires. Among the corpses of cult members, two were found to be pregnant, and 22 were kids, including a nine-month-old infant. In addition, 27 people were shot to death, including four kids. In the body of a child, bullets and shell fragments weighing 4.5 kilograms were collected.

The Evil Cult

The US government and media have never cited this type of act as a violation of religious freedom. Instead, they've gone the extra mile to repudiate the Chinese government for its crackdown on the evil cult, Falun Gong.

In the disguise of religion, the cult of Falun Gong exerts the spiritual control and belief autocracy upon its followers and has lured the public into its claws by saying the cult could protect people from disasters and diseases.

To date, more than 1,600 Falun Gong followers have been led to insanity, either injuring themselves or committing suicides. Some have died of diseases which would have been treated and cured had they consulted doctors in time.

It's rather justifiable for the Chinese government to crack down on the evil cult of Falun Gong to protect religious freedom, said the article.

However, thanks to diversity in human history and culture, productivity and social systems, religious situations vary across the world, and the measures taken by different countries to protect religious freedom could also differ.

"What we advocate here is a sincere and open dialogue between different religions and cultures rather than unwarranted charges or artificial confrontation."

"And countries should respect the diversity in human rights' developing modes and promote equal dialogue so as to deepen mutual understanding and settle disputes," the article said.

No practice should be allowed to interfere in another country's domestic affairs "in the name of defending religious freedom," and the article urged US government to respect the world's objective reality and abandon the practice of pursuing hegemony and power politics with the use of the religion issue.

Periodical Bibliography

The following articles have been selected to supplement the diverse views presented in this chapter.

Howard W. French   "Faith Sprouts in Arid Soil of China," *New York Times,* May 6, 2004.

Joseph Kahn   "Chinese Girls' Toil Brings Pain, Not Riches," *New York Times,* October 2, 2003.

Fang Lizhi   "China's Students: More Pro-Money than Pro-Democracy," *New Perspectives Quarterly,* Spring 2005.

David J. Lynch   "China Has Own Idea of Democracy," *USA Today,* October 10, 2003.

Robert Marquand   "Asian Democracy Blooms as China Watches," *Christian Science Monitor,* July 8, 2004.

Dean Peerman   "China Syndrome," *Christian Century,* August 10, 2004.

Dexter Roberts and Rose Brady   "In Rural China, Baby Steps Toward Democracy," *Business Week,* March 19, 2001.

Elizabeth Rosenthal   "In China, Catholic Churches Flourish, but Under Controls," *New York Times,* October 6, 2002.

Orville Schell   "China's Hidden Democratic Legacy," *Foreign Affairs,* July/August 2004.

Time   "A Leader Who Listens," June 27, 2005.

Jonathan Watts   "China and USA Row over Human Rights," *Lancet,* April 17, 2004.

Rebecca Weiner   "Wal-Mart, China, and Global Labor Rights," *Tikkun,* May/June 2005.

For Further Discussion

Chapter 1

1. The *Economist* and Philip Andrews-Speed both claim that China's energy and pollution problems are related to China's booming economy. Citing from the viewpoints, explain why China's leaders seem to be less concerned with these problems than with sustaining economic growth. What other factors do the authors claim might be holding up efforts to address these problems?

2. In the words of the *Lancet,* the government's response to the AIDS epidemic in China has been characterized by "denial, deception, and discrimination." To what other problems that China faces do the authors in this chapter make this charge against the Chinese government? In what viewpoints do the authors contend this charge is simply Western propaganda blown out of proportion? Which view do you find more persuasive? Why?

3. In Minxin Pei's view, the numerous and growing problems in China will soon lead to revolution. Do you agree with this view? If China's environmental problems, energy issues, tax burdens, and class divisions have been festering for decades, why do you think revolution has not already occurred? Explain your answers citing from the viewpoints in this chapter.

Chapter 2

1. John Wong and Sarah Chan believe that China can keep its economic juggernaut steaming forward. Bruce Gilley argues, however, that flaws in Chinese society will eventually arrest China's economic momentum. Whose argument do you find more convincing? Explain, addressing the various elements of China's economy and society that the authors use to support their arguments.

2. The viewpoints in this chapter concerning the U.S.-China trade deficit discuss China's export strength. Do you believe China is to blame for swamping America with cheap goods and thus taking away U.S. jobs? Explain your answer citing from the viewpoints.

3. Veronica Weinstein and Dennis Fernandez contend that China's efforts to combat intellectual property theft are sufficient to protect U.S. interests. Bruce Stokes disagrees and offers a confrontational method of pressuring China to stop intellectual property theft. Which strategies do you think will best protect U.S. interests? Explain, citing from the viewpoints.

Chapter 3

1. At the end of his viewpoint, Thomas M. Kane states, "If the PRC leaders do not feel that their external environment has changed, they have few reasons to change" their policy of building up their nuclear forces. Jeffrey Lewis counters that the Chinese are employing fewer nuclear weapons than they are actually capable of employing. Do you think this suggests that China's leaders are reacting to changes in their "external environment"? Explain why or why not.

2. After reading the Richard Halloran and Michael O'Hanlon viewpoints, explain what role the United States should play in China-Taiwan relations. Do you think America's leaders should counsel Taiwan against declaring independence? Do you think the United States should militarily defend Taiwan if it is attacked by mainland China? Under what circumstances should the United States act? Explain your answers citing from the viewpoints.

3. Do you think China's military, including its nuclear arsenal, is a serious threat to the United States? Citing from the viewpoints in this chapter, explain why or why not.

Chapter 4

1. According to the authors of several viewpoints in this chapter, the Chinese leadership is ardent in its commitment to making life better for its people. On the other hand, other authors in this chapter are suspect of how far the Communist Party is willing to take democratic reforms. What evidence in the viewpoints suggests that U.S. and Chinese commentators have a different notion of what democracy is?

2. In debates concerning human rights and religious freedom since the 1990s, commentators have consistently raised the name of the Falun Gong. China labels the religious group a "cult" and insists that its practices and doctrines threaten public well-being. Many Western spokespersons, however, believe the Falun Gong is merely a meditation sect that is being persecuted because it has a large membership and is a challenge to government authority. The Chinese government questions why the U.S. government opposes American cults, yet takes the side of the Falun Gong in its struggle with Beijing. What evidence do the authors provide to support their positions on the Falun Gong? Is the evidence provided sufficient to determine whether the Falun Gong is a cult? Explain, citing from the viewpoints.

3. Given what you have read in the viewpoints by Bei Ling and Andrea Huss and James Borton, in what ways do you think media freedom might help push China toward democracy? Borton writes that there is a force prompting more media freedom in China? Do you think this force will be a factor in China's continuing democratic reform? Is there evidence that this force is still not powerfulenough to thwart the government's control and censorship of media outlets? Explain your answers citing from the viewpoints.

Organizations to Contact

American Enterprise Institute (AEI)
1150 Seventeenth St. NW
  Washington, DC 20036
(202) 862-5800
Web site: www.aei.org

The institute is a public policy research organization dedicated to preserving and strengthening government, private enterprise, foreign policy, and national defense. Its Asian Studies Program focuses on the growing offensive capabilities of China's army, relations between Taiwan and mainland China, and economic and political reform in China. AEI's magazine, *American Enterprise*, often deals with developments in Asia, and the institute also publishes several books on China.

Amnesty International (AI)
5 Penn Plaza, 14th Fl.
  New York, NY 10001
(212) 807-8400
e-mail: admin-us@aiusa.org
Web site: www.amnesty.org

Amnesty International is an international organization that works to promote human rights. Every year AI issues reports on human rights progress in various countries, including China. It also publishes commentaries on human rights concerns specific to China. These papers are available on the organization's Web site.

Asia Society
725 Park Ave., New York, NY 10021
(212) 288-6400
e-mail: info@asiasoc.org
Web site: www.asiasociety.org

The Asia Society is an educational organization dedicated to fostering understanding of Asia and communication between Americans and the peoples of Asia and the Pacific Rim. Its AskAsia Web site (www.askasia.org) is an online information source for students interested in Asia studies. Reports such as "China: Fifty Years Inside the People's Republic" are available on the society's Web site.

Brookings Institution
1775 Massachusetts Ave. NW
  Washington, DC 20036
(202) 797-6000
Web site: www.brookings.org

Founded in 1927, the institution conducts research and analyzes global events and their impact on the United States and U.S. foreign policy. It publishes the quarterly *Brookings Review* as well as numerous books, including *The Rise of China and a Changing East Asian Order,* and various research papers on foreign policy.

CATO Institute
1000 Massachusetts Ave. NW
  Washington, DC 20001-5403
(202) 842-0200 • fax: (202) 842-3490
Web site: www.cato.org

The Cato Institute is a nonpartisan public policy research foundation that promotes the principles of limited government, individual liberty, and peace. Relations with China are a major research area within the institute's division of foreign policy studies. The institute publishes policy analysis reports and op-eds, including "China and the WTO" and "The Future of Liberalism in China."

Center for Security Policy
1920 L St. NW, Suite 210
  Washington, DC 20036
(202) 835-9077

e-mail: info@centerforsecuritypolicy.org
Web site: www.centerforsecuritypolicy.org

The center works to stimulate debate about all aspects of security policy, notably those policies bearing on the foreign, defense, economic, financial, and technology interests of the United States. It believes that China poses a threat to U.S. national security, and warns of this in many of its press releases and position papers.

Embassy of the People's Republic of China in the United States of America
2201 Wisconsin Ave. NW, Rm. 110
  Washington, DC 20007
(202) 338-6688 • fax: (202) 588-9760
Web site: www.china-embassy.org

The embassy posts news updates and white papers detailing the official Chinese government positions on such issues as Taiwan, China's entry into the World Trade Organization, and human rights. Its publications include the white papers "New Progress in China's Protection of Intellectual Property Rights" and "The Progress of Human Rights in China," which can be found on its Web site.

Freedom House
1319 Eighteenth St. NW
  Washington, DC 20036
(202) 296-5101 • fax: 202-296-5078
Web site: www.freedomhouse.org

Freedom House promotes human rights, democracy, free-market economics, the rule of law, and independent media around the world. It publishes *Freedom in the World*, an annual comparative assessment of the state of political rights and civil liberties in 191 countries.

Heritage Foundation
214 Massachusetts Ave. NE
  Washington, DC 20002-4999

(202) 546-4400 • fax: (202) 546-8328
Web site: www.heritage.org

The Heritage Foundation is a conservative think tank that formulates and promotes public policies based on the principles of free enterprise, limited government, individual freedom, traditional American values, and a strong national defense. It publishes many position papers on U.S.-China policy, such as "America's 'China Policy' Is in Urgent Need of Definition" and "Asia's Security Challenges."

Hoover Institution
Stanford University
   Stanford, CA 94305-6010
Web site: www-hoover.stanford.edu

The Hoover Institution is a public policy research center devoted to the advanced study of politics, economics, and political economy—both domestic and foreign—as well as international affairs. It publishes a newsletter and the quarterly *Hoover Digest*, which often includes articles on China.

Human Rights in China (HRIC)
350 Fifth Ave., Suite 3309
   New York, NY 10118
(212) 239-4495 • fax: (212) 239-2561
e-mail: hrichina@hrichina.org
Web site: www.hrichina.org

HRIC is an international nongovernmental organization founded by Chinese scientists and scholars. It monitors the implementation of international human rights standards in the People's Republic of China and carries out human rights advocacy and education among Chinese people inside and outside the country. HRIC's publications include the *China Rights Forum* as well as books, videotapes, and reports on the status of human rights in China.

Human Rights Watch
350 Fifth Ave., 34th Fl.
   New York, NY 10118-3299

(212) 290-4700 • fax: (212) 736-1300
e-mail: hrwnyc@hrw.org
Web site: www.hrw.org

The goal of Human Rights Watch, an international advocacy organization, is to raise awareness about human rights and to investigate and expose human rights violations. It publishes the *Human Rights Watch World Report 2005* as well as special reports on China such as "Freedom of Expression and the Internet in China."

Laogai Research Foundation

1925 K St., Suite 400, Washington, DC 20006
(202) 833-8770 • fax: (202) 833-6187
e-mail: laogai@laogai.org
Web site: www.laogai.org

The foundation is dedicated to collecting information about China's human rights abuses, including the use of forced labor camps, population control, and public executions. Its publications include the *Laogai Handbook* and various papers on human rights concerns, suppression of religious activity, and lack of Internet freedom in China.

Bibliography of Books

Deborah Z. Cass, Brett Williams, and George Robert Barker, eds.
China and the World Trading System: Entering the New Millennium. New York: Cambridge University Press, 2003.

Kim-Kwong Chan, Eric R. Carlson, and Brett G. Scharffs
Religious Freedom in China: Policy, Administration, and Regulation: A Research Handbook. Santa Barbara, CA: Institute for the Study of American Religion, 2005.

Jung Chang
Wild Swans: Three Daughters of China. New York: Touchstone, 2003.

Gregory C. Chow
Knowing China. River Edge, NJ: World Scientific, 2004.

Bruce Dalbrack
Broken Dragons: Crime and Corruption in Today's China. Hong Kong: Inkstone, 2004.

Neil J. Diamant, Stanley B. Lubman, and Kevin J. O'Brien, eds.
Engaging the Law in China: State, Society, and Possibilities for Justice. Stanford, CA: Stanford University Press, 2005.

Bruce J. Dickson
Red Capitalists in China: The Party, Private Entrepreneurs, and Prospects for Political Change. New York: Cambridge University Press, 2003.

Elizabeth C. Economy
The River Runs Black: The Environmental Challenge to China's Future. Ithaca, NY: Cornell University Press, 2005.

David Michael Finkelstein and Maryanne Kivlehan, eds.

China's Leadership in the 21st Century: The Rise of the Fourth Generation. Armonk, NY: M.E. Sharpe, 2003.

Ted C. Fishman

China, Inc.: How the Rise of the Next Superpower Challenges America and the World. New York: Scribner, 2005.

Rosemary Foot

Rights Beyond Borders: The Global Community and the Struggle over Human Rights in China. New York: Oxford University Press, 2000.

Bruce Gilley

China's Democratic Future: How It Will Happen and Where It Will Lead. New York: Columbia University Press, 2004.

Stephen Green and Guy S. Liu, eds.

Exit the Dragon? Privatization and State Control in China. Malden, MA: Blackwell, 2005.

Bruce Herschensohn

Across the Taiwan Strait: Democracy; The Bridge Between Mainland China and Taiwan. Lanham, MD: Lexington, 2002.

Chi Lo

When Asia Meets China in the New Millennium: China's Role in Shaping Asia's Post-Crisis Economic Transformation. Singapore: Pearson, 2003.

Constantine C. Menges

China: The Gathering Threat. Nashville: Nelson Current, 2005.

Françoise Mengin, ed.

Cyber China: Reshaping National Identities in the Age of Information. New York: Palgrave Macmillan, 2004.

National Academies   *Urbanization, Energy, and Air Pollution in China: The Challenges Ahead.* Washington, DC: National Academies Press, 2004.

Supachai Panitchpakdi and Mark L. Clifford   *China and the WTO: Changing China, Changing World Trade.* New York: John Wiley & Sons, 2002.

Michael Pillsbury   *China Debates the Future Security Environment.* Washington, DC: National Defense University Press, 2000.

Oded Shenkar   *The Chinese Century: The Rising Chinese Economy and Its Impact on the Global Economy, the Balance of Power, and Your Job.* Philadelphia: Wharton School, 2004.

Alvin Y. So   *China's Developmental Miracle: Origins, Transformations, and Challenges.* Armonk, NY: M.E. Sharpe, 2003.

Jonathan D. Spence   *The Search for Modern China.* New York: Norton, 2001.

John Bryan Starr   *Understanding China: A Guide to China's Economy, History, and Political Culture.* New York: Hill & Wang, 2001.

Robert L. Suettinger   *Beyond Tiananmen: The Politics of U.S.-China Relations, 1989–2000.* Washington, DC: Brookings Institution Press, 2004.

Robert G. Sutter   *China's Rise in Asia: Promises and Perils.* Lanham, MD: Rowman & Littlefield, 2005.

John J. Tkacik Jr., ed.   *Rethinking One China.* Washington, DC: Heritage Foundation, 2004.

Chaohua Wang, ed.   *One China, Many Paths.* New York: Verso, 2003.

Yiu-chung Wong   *From Deng Xiaoping to Jiang Zemin: Two Decades of Political Reform in the People's Republic of China.* Lanham, MD: University Press of America, 2005.

Index

abortions, forced, 190, 191
aerospace industry, 82, 84
Agreement on Trade-Related Intellectual Property Rights (TRIPS), 97, 98
agriculture, 16, 23, 28, 31, 186, 215
    production capabilities of, 20–21
AIDS. *See* HIV/AIDS
air force
    modernization of, 108–109
    nuclear capabilities of, 131–32
    in war with Taiwan, 158–59, 161, 162–64
air pollution, 26, 28, 37, 38
Aldhous, Peter, 37
Amnesty International, 187
Andrews-Speed, Philip, 33
Annual Report on the Military Power of the People's Republic of China (U.S. Department of Defense), 116
Argue, Don, 230
Asia, 74
    economic growth in, 16, 62, 64–65
    territorial disputes in, 125, 149, 173
    U.S. in, 116–17
Asia Times Online (Web publication), 214
atheism, 222

ballistic missile systems, modernization of, 109–10, 159
banking system, 75
Begert, William J., 121
Beijing Review (magazine), 133
Blair, Dennis, 121, 147, 153–54, 159

Borton, James, 211
Brown, Lester, 20
Bush, George H.W., 90, 93–95
Bush, George W., 125, 133, 221
    exaggerates China's nuclear capability, 135–37, 142–43
    Taiwan policy of, 146, 147–48, 153–56

Caijing (magazine), 212–13, 214–15, 216
Cai Zhuohua, 224
Campbell, Kurt, 146
cancer, 23
capitalism. *See* market economy
capital punishment, 193, 194
cars, 26, 73, 81–82, 84
Catholics, 192, 219–20, 223, 225
CDs, piracy of, 91
censorship, 201, 207–10, 212–17
Chan, Joseph, 216
Chan, Sarah, 61
Cheng Linsheng, 70
Chen Shui-bian, 152–53, 155
Chiang Kai-shek, 14–15, 148
Chile, 73
China's Democratic Future (Gilley), 14, 15
China's National Defense in 2002 (People's Republic of China white paper), 139
Chinese Embassy in the United States, 228
Chinese Military Power (U.S. Department of Defense), 140
Choate, Pat, 90–91, 92, 95
Chow, Gregory C, 18, 59, 214
Christians, 192, 219–20, 223, 224, 225, 230
Clinton, Bill, 90, 142
coal, dependence on, 26, 35–38
Cold War, 105

collective farms, 16, 20
Communist Party (CCP)
    alliance of, with nationalists,
        14–15
    decline of, 50–53
    membership of, 17, 176, 222
copyrighted materials. *See* intellec-
    tual property rights (IPR)
corruption, 213
    in government
        hinders economic growth,
            71–73, 75
        is being combated, 52, 173
        is major source of discon-
            tent, 183
        threatens public safety,
            73–74
    under nationalists, 14–15
Council on Foreign Relations, 129
cults, 223, 224–25, 232–33
cultural degradation, 74
currency policy, 86, 88

Daily Telegraph (newspaper), 125
death penalty, 193, 194
deforestation, 28
deLisle, Jacques, 179
democracy
    Communist Party is promot-
        ing, 171–78, 182, 185, 198–
        200
        con, 180–81, 182–84, 186
    economic growth and, 17–18,
        75–76, 171–72, 181–82
    Mao and, 15–16
    market economy requires, 71,
        73
    nationalists and, 14–15
    in Taiwan, 106, 148, 149,
        152–53
Democracy Movement of 1989,
    180–81, 182, 183
Deng Xiaoping, 16–17, 20, 184
Dickson, Bruce J., 17–18

Ding Zilin, 189
domestic violence, 190
Dong Yunhu, 229
Drezner, Daniel W., 208
DVDs, piracy of, 92
Dzokar, 195

economic growth, 27, 28, 49, 97,
    105
    democracy and, 17–18, 75–76,
        171–72, 181–82
    domestic demand drives, 64,
        65–66
    energy needs for, 37–38,
        62–63
    exports and, 64, 66–67
    multinational corporations
        and, 32, 83
    political reforms are necessary
        for continued, 70–73, 75
    rate of, 34–35, 59, 62–64, 174,
        175
    standard of living has in-
        creased with, 172–73, 174,
        175
    unevenness of, 15, 54, 55, 72,
        185–86
Economist (magazine), 22, 88
economy, 15, 49, 74
    under Deng, 16–17
    see also economic growth
Economy, Elizabeth, 28
education, 206
Eland, Ivan, 115
election system, 197, 201
energy
    consumption rates, 34–35
    decline in use of, 62–63
    dependence on coal for, 26,
        35–36, 38
    policy, 34, 36–41
English language, 206
environment, 32

government and, 23, 24–25, 29–31, 74

see also natural resources; pollution

Environmental Protection Bureaus, 29–30

epidemics, 43–45, 46, 188, 197–98, 216

Esarey, Ashley, 213–15

exports, 20

increase in, 17, 59, 66–67, 88, 172

expression, freedom of, 201, 207–10, 212–17

Falun Gong, 183, 207

as cult, 223, 224–25, 232, 233

mistreatment of adherents of, 220–21, 226–27

other religious groups and, 188, 191–92

family-planning policy, 20–21, 54, 168–69, 190, 191

Fargo, Thomas B., 146–47, 154

Farrell, Henry, 208

Feder, Jesse M., 92

Feng Chongyi, 76

Fernandez, Dennis, 96

foreign policy, 133

objectives, 124–25

One China principle and, 120, 148–50, 152, 173

Friedman, Edward, 76

gas, natural, shortage of, 34

Gill, Bates, 121

Gilley, Bruce, 14, 15, 69

Glaser, Bonnie S., 151

Goddess of Democracy, 180

government, 48, 53

accountability movement and, 185, 199

corruption in, 52, 71–74, 75, 183

environment and, 23, 24–25, 29–31, 74

health care and, 43, 45

intellectual property rights protection by, 93, 97–102

reform of, 70, 197–98, 199

is necessary, 49–50, 53–56

Greenpeace, 25

Gu Xianggao, 227

Halloran, Richard, 145

health, 23, 43, 174

care, costs of, 44–45, 46

He Shouming, 23

HIV/AIDS, 43, 188, 189

Hong Kong, 16, 65, 149, 173

Hot Property: The Stealing of Ideas in an Age of Globalization (Choate), 90

Hui community, 226

Hu Jintao, 17, 29, 133, 151, 183, 185

human rights abuses, 188–95, 201, 207–209

Human Rights Record of the US in 2004 (People's Republic of China white paper), 201

Hu Shuli, 212, 213, 215

Huss, Andrea, 205

income, 215

inequality of, 55, 72

India, 125

Indonesia, 65

industry, 16 63, 186

innovation is needed in, 70–71

safety in, 73–74

see also state-owned enterprises

Information Office (People's Republic of China), 196
intellectual property rights (IPR), 97–102
    piracy of U.S., 90–95, 97–98
intercontinental ballistic missiles (ICBMs), 129, 135, 140–42
International Covenant on Civil and Political Rights, 232
International Religious Freedom Act, 221
Internet censorship, 208, 214
Internet domain names, 99–100
Islam, 223, 225–26

Jane's Strategic Weapon Systems (journal), 136
Japan, 64, 116, 125
Jiang Zemin, 133, 170, 188, 207
    democracy and, 17, 183
    summit of, with George W. Bush, 147–48
judiciary, 201–202, 203

Kane, Thomas M., 123
Klein, Lawrence, 63
Knowing China (Chow), 18
Kong Youping, 191
Kuomintang, 14–15

labor unions, 189, 199–200
Lai, David, 120
Lancet (journal), 42
Lardy, Nicholas, 63
law, 49
    reform of, 188, 201–202, 203
    religion and, 219, 222–23, 229–34
law enforcement, 177–78
    abuses, 191, 193–94, 207, 226
    improvements in, 202–204
Lewis, Jeffrey, 134

Liao, Sarah, 31
Liao Yiwu, 209
Lieberthal, Kenneth, 29, 155
life expectancy, 174
Ling Bein, 205
Lin Yifu, 27
Liu Chengjun, 226
Liu Di 208
Liu Fenggang, 192
Liu Xiaobo, 207
Lobsang Tsering, 195

Macao, 149, 173
Ma Jun, 30
Malaysia, 65
Mao Zedong, 15–16, 20, 28, 127
market economy, 49
    decline of CCP and, 51–52
    democracy is requirement for successful, 71, 73
    under Deng, 16–17
middle class, 59, 181, 182
military modernization, 105
    is exaggerated, 116–22
mining, 23, 35, 36, 37
missile systems, 109–11, 113, 129–31, 132, 135–37, 140–42, 159
Mitchell, Derek, 146
movies, piracy of, 91
multinational corporations, 32, 83
    influence of, 87, 88
    in waste management, 23–24
Multiple Independently-targeted Reentry Vehicles (MIRVs), 130–31
Murray, Bruce, 29, 30
Muslims, 223, 225–26

National Development and Reform Commission (NDRC), 39
Nationalists, 14–15, 148
National Journal, 91

National People's Congress (NPC), 197

National Security Implications of the Economic Relationship between the United States and China (United States-China Security Review Commission), 116

natural resources, 28, 34, 74
water, 25–26, 30–31

naval forces, 160
modernization of, 112, 118–19, 119–20
nuclear capabilities of, 130, 131, 136–37

New York Times (newspaper), 141, 201

Nie Rongzhen, 138

Nike, 101–102

nongovernmental organizations, 185

nuclear weapons, are threat, 124–33
con, 135–44

O'Hanlon, Michael, 121, 157

oil, 34, 37, 125

Olympic Games, 32, 190

One China principle, 120, 148–50, 152, 173

one couple, one child policy, 20–21, 54, 168–69, 190, 191

Onyx, 23–24

"Opinions on Making Village Affairs Public and Improving the Democratic Management System" (State Council), 198

original equipment manufacturing (OEM), 101

Pakistan, 125

Pan Yue, 25–26, 28, 30

patent rights. *See* intellectual property rights

Payne, Keith, 143

Pei, Minxin, 47

People's Daily (newspaper), 151, 215

People's Liberation Army (PLA), 180
capabilities of, 119, 121, 126, 131–33, 160
modernization and restructuring of, 108, 110–12, 172

pharmaceuticals, piracy of, 90, 91–92, 95

Phuntsog Nyidrol, 221

political dissent, 180–81, 182, 183, 191, 209

pollution
air, 26, 28, 37, 38
government and, 23, 24–25, 29–31, 74
multinational corporations and, 23–24, 32
water, 25–26

population, 26, 28, 37, 45, 72, 149, 152
Communist Party and, 52, 176
family planning and, 20–21, 54, 168–69, 190, 191
in rural areas, 54, 168, 174

press, freedom of, 201, 207–10, 212–17

prisoners of conscience, 226–27, 231–32

prison system, 203–204

Protection of Intellectual Property Regulations (1995), 100

Protestants, 192, 219–20, 223, 224

Prueher, Joseph, 147

Qing dynasty, 14

Qu Geping, 28, 32

Rao Kegin, 45

rape, 190

Rawski, Thomas, 62–63
Red Capitalists in China (Dickson), 17–18
Re-education through Labour, 191, 194, 207, 226
Religious Affairs Bureau (RAB), 219–20
religious freedom, is restricted, 188, 191–92, 219–27
    con, 200, 219, 229–34
Roach, Stephen, 85, 88
Rumsfeld, Donald, 142
rural areas, 43, 44, 215
    building democracy in, 177, 182, 198–200
    population in, 54, 168, 174
    poverty in, 72, 186
    resistance to government in, 53–55
Russia
    as part of Soviet Union, 14, 105
    weapon systems from, 108–109, 112, 118

Sachs, Jeffrey D., 73
SARS (severe acute respiratory syndrome), 44, 183, 216
satellites, 113–14
Schaffer, Bob, 136
Scott, Robert E., 77
Shambaugh, David, 117, 120
Sha Zukang, 174
Singapore, 16, 65
software, piracy of, 91, 92, 93, 94, 101
South Korea, 65, 74, 116–17
space technology development, 113–14, 130
speech, freedom of, 199
standard of living, 172–73, 174, 175
State Administration for Religious Activities (SARA), 219–20, 222

State Council, 198
State Economic and Trade Commission (SETC), 39
State Environmental Protection Administration (SEPA), 29–30
state incapacitation, 53
state-owned enterprises, 23, 38–40, 59, 72, 171
State Planning Commission (SPC), 39
Steorts, Jason Lee, 224
Stokes, Bruce, 89
submarine-launched ballistic missiles (SLBMs), 130, 136–37
Sudan, 125
Sun Jian, 26–27, 30
Sun Yat-sen, 14

Taiwan, 153
    democracy in, 106, 148, 149, 152–53
    economy of, 16, 65, 150
    possibility of war with, 106, 146–48, 151–56, 158–64
    unification with, 120, 148–50
Taiwan Relations Act (1979), 154
Tanks, David, 137
tax collection, 54–55
territorial expansion, 120, 148–50, 152, 173
textile industry, 80–81, 87
Thailand, 65
Three Grades of Servants Church, 227
Tiananmen Mothers, 189
Tiananmen Square protests, 180, 183
Tibet, repression in, 194–95
Tilelli, John, 136
de Tocqueville, Alexis, 55
Togliatti, Palmiro, 127
Topden, 195
trade

intellectual property rights and, 93–95, 97–102
policies of China, harm U.S., 78–84
con, 86–88
trademark rights. *See* intellectual property rights
trade unions, 189, 199–200

Uighur community, 194, 220, 223, 226
United States, 201
China's trade policies harm, 78–84
con, 86–88
in East Asia, 116–17
military of, 105, 119, 121, 142
savings in, 87, 88
studies of Chinese military, 116, 130–33, 135, 136–41
war over Taiwan and, 106, 146–48, 151–56, 164–65
see also specific presidents
United States–China Security Review Commission, 116
U.S. Commission on International Religious Freedom (USCIRF), 229
U.S. Department of Defense, 107, 116, 140
U.S. Department of State, 218

vehicles, 26, 73, 81–82, 84

Wall, Robert, 113
Wal-Mart, 94
Wang Chaohua, 184
Wang Jianqin, 74
Wang Jianshuo, 208
Wang Yiliang, 209
Wan Li, 71
Washington Times (newspaper), 135

waste disposal, 23–24, 26
water, 25–26, 30–31
weapons systems, 121
domestic production of, 117–18
modernization of, 109–11, 113
needed to seize Taiwan, 158, 159
nuclear, are threat, 124–33
con, 135–44
from Russia, 108–109, 112, 118
Weinstein, Veronica, 96
Wen Jiabao, 183, 185, 221
environment and, 29, 32
Who Will Feed China? (Brown), 20
Wing Thye Woo, 73
Wolf, Charles, Jr., 72
women, violence against, 168, 190–91
Wong, John, 61
workplace accidents, 37, 73–74
World Trade Organization (WTO), 78, 153
increase in exports and, 17, 59
intellectual property rights obligations of members of, 90, 92, 97
Wu Jianguo, 128

Xie Qingkui, 73
Xinjiang Autonomous Region, 194, 220, 223, 226
Xiong Lei, 45
Xu Wenli, 209
Xu Yonghai, 192

Yang, Xiaokai, 73
Yang Huan, 127–28
Ye Guozhu, 190

Yi Minhong, 206
Yu, Frank, 208

Zhang Lei, 70
Zhang Shengqi, 192

Zhao Bingli, 168
Zhao Nanqi, 125
Zhong Gong movement, 223
Zhu Rongji, 26, 28, 29, 71
Zweig, David, 149